JOURNALISM ETHICS

Philosophical Foundations
for News Media

JOURNALISM ETHICS

PHILOSOPHICAL FOUNDATIONS FOR NEWS MEDIA

John C. Merrill
University of Missouri–Columbia

Bedford/St. Martin's
Boston ◆ New York

Sponsoring editor: Suzanne Phelps Weir
Managing editor: Patricia Mansfield Phelan
Project editor: Diane Schadoff
Production supervisor: Melissa Kaprelian
Art director: Lucy Krikorian
Graphics: Huron Valley Graphics, Inc.
Cover design: Evelyn Horovicz

Library of Congress Catalog Card Number: 96-67624

Manufactured in the United States of America.

1 0 9 8 7
f e d c

For information, write:
Bedford/St. Martin's
75 Arlington Street
Boston, MA 02116
(617-399-4000)

ISBN: 0–312–13899–7

CONTENTS

Contents

Contents

Contents

Contents

LIST OF FIGURES

PREFACE

This is a book about journalism ethics. Beyond that, it is a book about the philosophical foundations of journalism morality. It is also a book that suggests a moderate approach to ethics in journalism—a position that I am calling *ethical mutualism,* which is summed up in the final chapter.

Many other journalism ethics books are case oriented. This one is not. Rather, it is what I like to call a mega-issue book because it considers the foundations that underlie specific cases and microissues such as journalists taking gifts or moonlighting during off-hours. At the end of each chapter and in the Appendix, however, issues are included (with questions), which can provide the stimuli for classroom discussion or written assignments. A Glossary of important terms is also included at the end of the book.

Another feature of *Journalism Ethics* is the Foundational Mentor boxes, which are found throughout. In addition, the student will find a number of figures that capsulize some of the major concepts discussed in the various chapters. Basic philosophical orientations have an impact on ethical reasoning and acting. Therefore, this book discusses some of these orientations for students' consideration. The most prominent of these are *individualism* and *communitarianism* and the accompanying concepts of freedom and responsibility.

Such foundational considerations as journalistic truth and its relationships to ethics are discussed. The dark side of ethics—

propaganda—is given particular emphasis, probably for the first time in a journalism ethics book. A scourge of good journalism—Machiavellianism—is taken up in the chapter on propaganda. There is also a chapter on general semantics, which provides journalism students with helpful ways to think about language and its relationship to thought and action. Readers will find some insights into ancient Chinese philosophy as well.

Fairness is another foundational ethical concept. It is a very complex one in that it impinges on the normal journalistic goal of objective reporting. Does the journalist report forthrightly and fully? Or does the journalist consider possible consequences and tamper with the facts of the story in the name of fairness? Questions such as these are dealt with in Chapter 8.

Theories of ethics are discussed in an early chapter. I have, for the purposes of this book, presented two main theories, *pragmatic* and *humanistic*, with the latter of these (the most important) comprising three subtheories: the deontological (exemplified by Kant), the teleological (exemplified by J. S. Mill), and the personalist (exemplified by Kierkegaard). It is hoped that this discussion of theories will provide students with a systematic way to consider various ethical actions and will help them realize that several legitimate ethical roads may be taken.

Journalism Ethics tries to get students to think about issues and concepts and to acquaint them with the parallels and paradoxes related to journalism ethics. Instead of focusing on the daily routine of journalism, it focuses on the philosophy and theoretical foundations that *support* that daily routine. If students will read this book with half the seriousness and concern with which it has been written, lights should flash in the darkness of mundane academic busywork and students will be off to read a good newspaper and to take a look at the works of thinkers such as Confucius, Aristotle, Kant, Locke, Sissela Bok, and Alasdair MacIntyre. What more could an author wish?

Finally, I would like to thank my editor at St. Martin's Press,

Preface

Suzanne Phelps Weir, my project editor, Diane Schadoff, and my copy editor, Judy Voss, for their fine work. Additional thanks go to the following reviewers for their helpful comments: William Click, Winthrop University; Mike Cowling, University of Wisconsin; and John Ginn, University of Kansas.

John C. Merrill

JOURNALISM ETHICS

Philosophical Foundations
for News Media

CHAPTER ONE

NEEDED:
A MORE ETHICAL PRESS

One thing we know: Criticism of the media is crashing in from all sides. Journalism and its practitioners increasingly are being cast as social villains, dispensing superficial, negative, and sensational information harmful to the health of society. The Hutchins Commission, which studied the press during and just after World War II, handed down its report in 1947: It reproached journalism for being socially irresponsible. Since then, a succession of critics has stressed the need for a more responsible press. Television especially has shown little concern for responsible programming that would encourage civility, thoughtfulness, and morality. Television's Jim Lehrer has excoriated journalism for its arrogance and its "lousy and snide" practices; such indictments are becoming the norm. What can be done about the problems? More concern for ethics may at least be a partial answer.

As we begin to consider the philosophical foundations of journalism ethics, we should first look at the present state of the press and at why there is concern. What are the main problem areas in relations between the public and the media? Numerous surveys in recent years have shown that the public has little faith in, or respect for, the press. Actually, as Michael J. Robinson and Norman Ornstein (1990, 34) have pointed out, it is not so much that the people dislike the press (they seem to have affection for it in a general sense), but that, in increasing numbers, they do not believe it.

Professor Charles Self (1988, 17) of Texas A&M University examined the reasons for public distrust of the media and of the journalists working for them. He found that there are four main reasons for the credibility gap:

1. Insensitivity, arrogance, and generally bad behavior by journalists
2. Inaccuracies, incompleteness, and generally poor professional practices
3. Disagreements over the kinds of news used and over news judgment
4. Disagreements over the task of news in the lives of readers

Certainly there are many other reasons, some perhaps as important as these, for the public's loss of faith in the press. If the main purpose of the mass media is to water the roots of democracy by helping to create a knowledgeable and sensitive electorate, then the overabundance of sleaze, rumor, gossip, sensation, superficiality, and arrogance does not bode well for responsible journalism. Leo Bogart (1995, 1–2), writing about the media's relationship to democracy, notes that the situation does not look too promising. He writes: "A sober look at how media work in today's world suggests that they remain vulnerable to manipulation—by political authorities motivated by ideological zeal or crude self-interest, or by economic forces that limit their resources, their variety and their integrity. They are not inevitably an agent of democracy."

A common theme in the public's criticism of the media is that the concept of freedom has gotten out of hand and that the media push all sorts of irresponsible information in the name of freedom of the press. Responsible journalism, not free journalism, is increasingly proposed by would-be media reformers. As we will see in the following section, the old ideas of the Enlightenment philosophy are increasingly being questioned.

A Problem: Enlightenment Liberalism

The new communitarians (who stress social responsibility) believe that the basic cause for the public's current distrust of the press is that journalism is still mired in the Enlightenment's liberal ideas of individualism and libertarianism. The public sees only inconsistency in media practices; it sees no core of virtuous agreement and no shared sense of responsibility among journalists. Thus, the public begins to doubt whether there are *any* common ethical standards in journalism. It seems, to the public, that all journalism is relative and that the press is following John Stuart Mill's belief that the "only freedom which deserves the name is that of pursuing our own good in our own way" (Merrill, 1994, ch. 16).

Communitarian critics of the modern American press see such Enlightenment liberalism (or libertarianism) as an individualist mind-set that is counterproductive to a meaningful ethics and that deprecates the spirit of cooperation and community progress. Michael Sandel (1984, 1), for one, bemoans the relativism found in liberalism and asks: "Why should toleration and freedom of choice prevail when other important values are also at stake?"

Stephen Holmes (1993), discussing liberalism and its enemies, provides a good look at writers who echo Sandel's perspective. Holmes points out that although liberalism's opposition to interference with the individual's life is well entrenched in the Western mind, the opposition to liberalism is also a tradition. It is represented, he says, by such modern figures as Sandel, Joseph de Maistre, Leo Strauss, Alasdair MacIntyre, Amitai Etzioni, and Christopher Lasch. These *antiliberals*

3

(communitarians) stress the social nature of human beings and view liberalism as atomistic, that is, regarding each person as a separate, self-contained entity. The antiliberals also emphasize that values are absolute; many of them put stress on God and the supreme value of religious authority, and in so doing, they are critical of liberalism for its moral relativism and secularism.

Holmes, who teaches political theory at the University of Chicago, shows that the great liberal writers, such as John Locke, Adam Smith, and John Stuart Mill—men who significantly influenced Western journalism—were insightful and well-balanced thinkers who did not make the kind of errors attributed to them by the antiliberals. They were not, for example, so extreme in their individualism as to ignore or deny the importance of a person's living in society and relating to other people. The idea that human beings can be fully human only as members of tightly knit social groups goes back at least to the philosophy of Plato. Today this notion has been influentially represented by late-twentieth-century writers such as Robert Bellah and Alasdair MacIntyre.

One truth ignored in such communitarian critiques of liberalism, contends Holmes, is that many cohesive social groups are evil, and if individualism means standing apart from such groups, then individualism can be quite a good thing. Reporters who, due to their individual consciences, refuse to go along with the group-mandated activities of their newspapers, are not necessarily wrong in ethics and may very well be right. At any rate, we see that the deep strain of individualism, although lessening, can still be found in American journalism and that it still results in a pluralism of ethical perspectives.

Journalist Michael J. O'Neill (1993, 193) points to the weaknesses of modern mass media (especially television) and fires this blast at journalists: "They should be looking past today's breaking news to discover the hidden pockets of misunderstanding, the undetected human tensions that will burst into the headlines tomorrow, next week, or a month or year from now."

Reflecting the communitarian ethos, O'Neill stresses that journalism should be "preventive rather than merely reactive" (193–94), and he faults journalism for serving entertainment rather than thought:

> Immediate action and controversy are the dominant fare at most newspapers, and superficiality bathed in entertainment and fiction is the chief product of television. The media's mission to inform democracy would be better served if they redefined news to emphasize thought as well as action, harmony as well as conflict, explanation as well as exposure. . . . This kind of journalism would search out the causes of social breakdowns before they turn into the failures and violence which the TV shows now celebrate.

The popular British writer C. S. Lewis had very little good to say about the press. Normally calm and scholarly in his writing style, Lewis produced heat when he denounced the newspapers. James Heiser (1992, 51) quotes Lewis as writing these blunt words to a friend: "I never read the papers. Why does anyone? They're nearly all lies, and one has to wade thru such reams of verbiage and 'write up' to find out even what they're saying."

According to Heiser (52), Lewis's contempt for the press was due to his rejection of "wicked journalists"—people "who disseminate for money falsehoods calculated to produce envy, hatred, suspicion and confusion." Lewis believed that what little respect the press may have is due to the fact that many researchers rely on newspapers for their information. But this respectability of the press is perpetuated by circular logic: A researcher uses a particular newspaper because of its authority, but the reason that it is authoritative is because many scholars use it.

Lewis stated that "we must get rid of our arrogant assumption that it is the masses who can be led by the nose. As far as I can make out, the shoe is on the other foot." Lewis continued: "The only people who are really the dupes of their favourite newspapers are the *intelligentsia*. It is they who read leading articles [editorials]: the poor read the sporting news, which is mostly true" (Heiser, 53).

Television, perhaps even more than the press, provides a diet of sensation, sleaze, negativism, and superficial news coverage. S. I. and Alan R. Hayakawa (1993) discuss the weaknesses of the television medium—especially its limited and distorted picture of reality, which they call the "world through the keyhole." The authors describe television's "advocacy of individual gratification through romance and consumption of material goods" (147) and note that it is "not balanced by advocacy of thrift or of work."

There are, the Hayakawas say, a few excellent television shows (such as Robin MacNeil's series, *The Story of English*), but these "few bright moments on the small screen" are the exception. The authors conclude (154): "If humanity had used writing in the same limited way we use television, we would have created for ourselves little more than tabloid newspapers and comic books."

Recent Warnings on the Ethical Front

The erosion of press believability extends to all media, but especially to television from which the people say they get most of their news. Robinson and Ornstein (1990) did show, however, that network anchors were rated as more believable than such nonjournalists at the time as Donald Trump, Mikhail Gorbachev, Johnny Carson, and George Bush. They also found that daily newspapers' believability had fallen a full sixteen points in five years. This problem of credibility is extremely important, especially to journalists. If their stories cannot be believed, then the whole of journalism is on a shaky foundation.

A 1994 survey conducted in eight Western democracies indicated a deep skepticism about the growing "tabloidization" of the news media. In Britain, for example, 23 percent of the people said that the press *hurts* democracy rather than helps it (Tucher and Bischoff, 1995, 161). And only 49 percent of the British respondents saw the press as good for democracy. The image or reputation of the press as a serious and helpful social institution seems to be dissolving everywhere in the world. Tabloidism is largely responsible for this, and, as was noted in 1995, if "that's what it takes to sell newspapers, the next Gallup poll will leave the journalists providing consolation for the car salesmen" (Tucher and Bischoff, 162).

The 1993 Gallup poll was bad enough. It found that less than a third of Americans believed that journalists had high ethical standards (Henry, 1993). In the same year, *USA Today* apologized for a "misleading" picture showing armed Los Angeles youth-gang members ready to retaliate if Los Angeles police officers were acquitted of beating Rodney King. The printing of the picture certainly did not help the media's image. Nor was it helped by other incidents, such as the rigged GM truck explosion aired by NBC News, also in 1993, or the television reporter and cameraman in Minnesota who admitted giving alcohol to a minor to illustrate a story on teenage drinking. In 1995, the circus atmosphere created by the press in the O. J. Simpson trial did little to help the media's image. Another media problem that year involved Connie Chung and Newt Gingrich's mother. During the taping of a CBS show, Chung had assured Newt Gingrich's mother that revealing Newt's opinion of Hillary Clinton ("she's a bitch") would be "between you and me." Chung betrayed this promise, and the story went international.

Many newspeople believe that such incidents have led to a new ethical awareness—even a moral renewal—among journalists across the country. For instance, Don Browne of NBC

News has argued that the network's trauma over the GM controversy actually gave a boost to ethical concern in newsrooms everywhere (Henry, 1993, 54). His exact words: "Journalism will not be diminished but strengthened. Because we made one mistake on *Dateline NBC*, hundreds of mistakes will *not* be made elsewhere." But Henry (54) contends that news consumers have serious doubts about whether journalistic ethical concern has been enhanced.

Henry says that although individual journalists may have "highly developed ethical sensibilities," journalism as a whole—unlike law or medicine—has no licensing, no disciplining boards, and no generally accepted codes of behavior. He points out that such actions as undercover exposés of wrongdoing are acceptable by some media and forbidden by others. And, he adds, in most media nothing is automatically a firing offense (54). Editors, Henry notes, insist on dealing with every case individually, and this leads to a kind of permissiveness.

The press came under a torrent of criticism for overplaying and biasing the coverage of the 1993 siege and explosive attack near Waco, Texas, on the religious sect (Branch Davidians) led by David Koresh. Television coverage of this incident was considered particularly inflammatory. A "feeding frenzy" by the media? Many journalists believe such coverage is just that. Others, however, do not agree, believing stories of celebrities and titillating court cases are quite natural and expected by the audience. These journalists say that it is the public, not the press, who must take most of the blame for a "feeding frenzy," if such a frenzy in fact exists.

Guilt within the Press

This "blame the public" type of rationalization notwithstanding, there is a growing sense of guilt within the media. Journalists' concern with their possible excesses was evident in a story

(Quindlen, 1994) in which a number of media personalities were asked to express their opinions. Typical of the sins mentioned in the story were these comments by Jeff Greenfield and Lesley Stahl, who are television reporters, and Michael Kinsley, who is in both television and the print media:

GREENFIELD: "[There] is the difficulty of insulating yourself from prurience. . . . I think what's happened now is that a lot of the most appalling stuff is right in your face—as easy to reach as a flick of the channel. You can turn off an evening news program and you're right into 'Hard Copy' or 'Montel' or 'Sally Jessy' " (28).

STAHL: "I think what we're all dancing around is that journalism hasn't caught up with the technology we're using. You can throw a guy on the air live. You haven't any thought, in your own mind, about what you're going to do once he opens his mouth. We don't check anything out until it's out there. And once it's out there, the talk show hosts get it and the tabloids get it and then we say, 'Oh, my God, we're being forced to run that' " (31).

KINSLEY: "What about the hypocrisy of the viewers and the readers? They say they don't like us; they're disgusted with the press for covering all this sleaze, and then they create a market for it. That's why it feeds the fire" (53).

Whereas Kinsley is prone to shift the blame to the audience, another well-known broadcaster, Jim Lehrer of the *Newshour*, excoriates the contemporary press (1993, 3), saying he knows of no time in American history in which journalism has been practiced so poorly. He goes on to say: "Journalism in my opinion is being consumed before our eyes and ears by a form of arrogance that I believe, if it is not arrested and stopped soon, could undermine the whole point of the exercise."

Lehrer urges people not to "tolerate lousy, arrogant, snide journalism," to cease reading newspapers and watching television news programs that are irresponsible and arrogant. Paul H. Weaver (1994), a former Harvard political science professor, also severely censures the press and contends, like Lehrer, that the failings of the news business today seriously threaten American constitutional democracy. He, too, suggests a boycott of modern journalism in general by right-thinking citizens.

Other journalists have pointed to the arrogant and hypersensitive demeanor of the press. Howard Kurtz (1993, 33), a reporter for the *Washington Post*, writes: "Although news organizations make their living pointing fingers and hurling accusations, they are notoriously slow to fess up to their own mistakes. With varying degrees of stubborness, stupidity, and arrogance, media executives often circle the wagons when their own actions come under scrutiny."

In 1994, at the onset of the O. J. Simpson case, the prestigious journal of Harvard's Nieman Foundation, *Nieman Reports*, published a special issue called "Ethics of Trial," in which many writers dealt with current ethical problems in journalism. The titles of a number of the articles show journalists' concern with ethical improvement: "Tonya Harding Orgy," "Michael Jackson Scandal," "TV Sitting on Stories to Improve Ratings," "Presuming They Know the Truth," "Indians Struggle on in Battle for Fairness," "Can Militant Minority Reporters Be Objective?" "The Ombudsman As Ethicist," "Who Cares about the Truth?" and "Surrender of the Gatekeepers."

This special issue of *Nieman Reports* on ethics was appropriately subtitled "Tabloid Trash and Flash Threaten to Corrupt the American Media." One of the authors, Katherine Fulton, a former North Carolina editor who now teaches at Duke University, had these harsh words to say about journalists: "Our [journalists'] performance has led to a deepening credibility problem, which in turn feeds the desire some people have to bypass mainstream journalism and search for other information sources. We're arrogant, we're ignorant, we're destructive. If citizens are disengaged from politics, our cynicism is partly to blame. This litany from inside and outside the profession is familiar—and mostly ignored in the nation's newsrooms" (17).

Much of the media's arrogance may stem from a smug feeling of being protected by the First Amendment, from a recognition of their power, and from the fact that they have the last word in most controversies. Press power, of course, can be counterproductive to ethical action. Here is what Professor Ted J. Smith (1992, 30) of Virginia Commonwealth University says on this point:

> American democracy is founded on the idea that no group, no matter how enlightened or altruistic, should be able to exercise unrestrained power. Journalists constitute a tiny, homogeneous, and closed elite. They are also enormously powerful, thanks to an unplanned and unforeseen sequence of developments that placed them in control of the most effective means of communication in a mass democracy. As long as it was restrained by stringent professional norms of objectivity and balance, that power could be tolerated. Without those norms, it is intolerable.

Columnist William Safire (1994, 4A) has pointed out that the media too often treat public figures unfairly. He referred specifically to the 1994 Cardinal Joseph Bernardin case, in which the Roman Catholic prelate in Chicago was accused by Steven Cook of sexually molesting him years earlier. Cook, under hypnosis, had "recovered" memories of the supposed abuse. Four months later, Cook admitted his memory was not reliable and dropped the $10 million lawsuit. According to Safire, "the Bernardin episode raises acute ethical questions for lawyers and journalists." Although the lawsuit was "without a whisper of credible evidence to support it," the media treatment of it resulted in a "devastating assault on the character of a public man of high reputation."

Safire notes that "responsible journalism is not stenography" but requires judgment about the credibility of sources and claims. The media should have learned, writes Safire, in the heyday of Senator Joe McCarthy, "that it was not honest to keep reporting his charges without putting them in the context of his record." The Bernardin case, says Safire, suggests that the lesson must be relearned.

Other leading ethical controversies in recent years have centered on such press practices as tampering with quotes, omitting the names of sources, staging news photographs, impersonating someone to get a story, paying for interviews with newsmakers, intentionally biasing stories, and using sexist or racist language. American journalists have differing opinions about the rights and wrongs of these and the many other ethical problems found daily in their work.

Many journalists, though, believe the problem lies in the absence of a universal, absolute standard for the practice of journalism. This premise is, in fact, the driving force behind the communitarians, just as it was the underlying concern of the Hutchins Commission in its study of the American press a half century ago. We should look briefly at the Commission's ideas about a responsible press; they have been resurrected in large part by the modern-day communitarians.

The Need for a Responsible Press

Although the need for a more responsible press is increasingly expressed in our society, such a "need" has been discussed since the earliest days of the republic. The Founding Fathers talked about it after a rather scurrilous party journalism established itself in the new country. In every era, voices have cried out against press irresponsibility. Since World War II, such voices have had wide circulation and stimulated considerable dialog and controversy, especially in academic circles. Prior to the 1950s, the American press focused almost exclusively on its freedom guaranteed by the First Amendment, but during the last five decades the emphasis has shifted to journalistic responsibility. The principal agent in this shift of emphasis has been the report of the Hutchins Commission, which was published in 1947. Even though the majority of practicing journalists may not have encountered the Hutchins report firsthand, its concepts and criticisms have filtered into their world. Prior to the Hutchins report, many journalists and academicians had thought in terms of "responsibility," but no significant effort had been made to consider the concept as a serious theory parallel in importance to "libertarianism." Before 1947, if responsibility in journalism was considered at all, it was thought of as being automatically built into a libertarian press, or it was assumed that various media would interpret "responsibility" in their own ways. In other words, the many interpretations of responsibility were considered a sign not only of a free press but also of a responsible press.

Hutchins (see box, p. 14) and his twelve commissioners thought differently. They saw a very clear danger in the restriction of communication outlets and general irresponsibility in many areas of American journalism. Consequently, their report offered the ominous warning that if the mass media persist in being irresponsible, "not even the First Amendment will protect their freedom from governmental control" (80).

The Hutchins Commission Revisited

Two main conclusions stood out in the Hutchins report: (1) that the press has a responsibility to society; and (2) that the libertarian press of the United States was not meeting its responsibility. Therefore, a need for a new journalistic theory (or emphasis) existed.

For a few years after the report came out, the majority of American publishers were angry about it and the authoritarian implications they read in (or into) it. By the mid-1950s, how-

FOUNDATIONAL MENTOR

Robert Maynard Hutchins (1899–1977)

A lawyer-philosopher by training and inclination, Robert M. Hutchins, as chancellor of the University of Chicago and chairman of the influential Commission of Freedom of the Press in the 1940s, had a profound impact on the philosophical foundations of American journalism. He and his twelve commissioners studied the press at the end of World War II, found it basically socially irresponsible, and made suggestions for its improvement. The Commission's report was published in 1947 as *A Free and Responsible Press*. This book and subsequent discussion of it in press and academic circles marked a paradigm shift in journalistic emphasis: from press freedom to press responsibility.

The Commission's study was the brainchild of Henry Luce, publisher of *Time* and *Life,* who largely funded the project and recruited Hutchins to be its chairman. Hutchins had long considered the press an essential social institution, especially in the area of continuing education, and was happy to accept the assignment. He appointed the twelve members of the commission, all of whom were leading intellectuals and nonjournalists.

Although Hutchins was extremely interested in press freedom, he visualized it mainly as a freedom "to do good"—a kind of positive freedom tied to a responsibility to advance social progress. He warned that if the press is not responsible, it will "suddenly find that forces in soci-

ever, the issue had largely settled down, with journalists perhaps thinking that the best policy was to ignore the report. But the report did not go away. Its ideas gradually took root in journalism, as there was already a readiness to challenge the old ideas of individualism and pluralistic freedom.

14

continued

ety, perhaps the government, will deprive it of its liberty" (NBC/Univ. of Chicago broadcast, April 6, 1947).

Press responsibility was the main theme of his Commission's study. In order to be responsible, according to the Commission, the press should cease publishing so much trivia and gossip and should refrain from its basic negative and sensational orientation. It should engage in more self-criticism and welcome more external criticism. The Commission saw the press as too sensitive, too profit-oriented, and as failing to provide society with enough significant information in a meaningful context. The press was also criticized for neglecting many ideas of society's constituent groups and for being entirely too inward looking and superficial.

Robert Hutchins was not popular with the press, which considered his ideas a threat to freedom. He and his commissioners were seen as ignorant of the problems of journalism and unrealistic in their criticisms. But, in spite of considerable continuing anti-Hutchins animosity, the American press bears Hutchins's stamp of increased social consciousness. Undoubtedly, if Hutchins were here today, he would still not like the overall quality of the press, but he would see many of the changes he suggested some half century ago and would hope that the spirit of the new communitarianism would bring even more changes.

The best researched and strongest worded book blasting the Hutchins Commission report was published in 1950 by Chicago journalist Frank Hughes. He criticized the report and the "arrogance" of the Commission, its lack of members who were journalists, and its inherent authoritarianism. By 1956 the heat had largely disappeared from discussions of the Hutchins report. It was in that year that University of Illinois journalism professors Fred Siebert, Theodore Peterson, and Wilbur Schramm published their popular book, *Four Theories of the Press.* From this work the new "theory" of social responsibility made its way, largely unchallenged, into innumerable books, articles, speeches, classrooms, and academic theses and dissertations.

This new theory was depicted as an outgrowth of the libertarian theory, not just a change in emphasis. Its acceptance was aided by the common suspicion of, and dissatisfaction with, the libertarianism of *press-centered* journalism. Implicit in this trend toward social responsibility was the loss of faith in the Enlightenment concept that people (journalists included) are rational and quite capable of deciding what is responsible. Again, there was the Platonic idea that some arbiter, some authority, some group, or some kind of philosopher-king is needed to define how the media should be responsible. This incipient seed of monolithic responsibility is what has continued to disturb many media people, who retain a basic belief in pluralism and libertarianism.

The Hutchins Commission went beyond the libertarians in that it stressed what the press *should* do. In this way, it was beginning to plow a relatively new field in journalism: ethics. And, as journalism professor Edmund Lambeth (1992) has noted, the legacy of the Hutchins Commission persists. He states that many media leaders are "finding the nomenclature of 'social responsibility' irresistible," and "countless classrooms consider and some even memorize its injunctions" (7). Even though it may be true, as Lambeth says, that the Commission's literature "contains little that would assist individual journalists in daily ethical judgments" (7), it did take a giant step away from libertarianism and thrust journalistic thinking into a different ("social" or "communitarian") direction.

Needed: A More Ethical Press

Press Responsibility: The Requirements

The Hutchins Commission (20–29) came up with five requirements for the press if it is to be responsible to the society:

1. *The media should provide a truthful, comprehensive, and intelligent account of the day's events in a context which gives them meaning.* (Media should be accurate; they should not lie, should separate fact from opinion, should report in a meaningful way internationally, and should go beyond the facts and report the truth.)

2. *The media should serve as a forum for the exchange of comment and criticism.* (Media must be common carriers; they must publish ideas contrary to their own, "as a matter of objective reporting"; all "important viewpoints and interests" in the society should be represented; media must identify sources of their information for this is "necessary to a free society.")

3. *The media should project a representative picture of the constituent groups in the society.* (When images presented by the media fail to present a social group truly, judgment is perverted; truth about any group must be representative; it must include the group's values and aspirations, but it should not exclude the group's weakness and vices.)

4. *The media should present and clarify the goals and values of the society.* (Media are educational instruments; they must assume a responsibility to state and clarify the ideals toward which the community should strive.)

5. *The media should provide full access to the day's intelligence.* (There is a need for the "wide distribution of news and opinion.")

The Requirements: Some Questions

Few of us would deny the nobility of the spirit that underlies the requirements formulated by the Hutchins Commission. Some libertarians, however, might wince at the thought

17

of these things being *required* in some way, which was the implication behind the Commission's report. Nevertheless, the five media duties are generally consistent with journalistic ethics of any serious type. There are, however, some questions that thoughtful students might ask and discuss. Here are a few of them, keyed to the five requirements:

1. Can the media actually present a truthful account of the day's events, much less a comprehensive and intelligent one? And how can media put all these events into a meaningful context? Is this a completely unrealistic—even naive—requirement or expectation for the media?

2. Do not, and have not, the media always *to some degree* served as a forum for the exchange of comment and criticism? Just what did the Commission mean by this requirement? Was it simply saying that the media should do more in this respect? How much comment and criticism is enough? What kind of comment and criticism should there be?

3. How can the media project a representative picture of the constituent groups in the society? It is doubtful that the media can *even identify* all the constituent groups, much less give a representative picture of them.

4. Is it not too much to ask of the press to present and clarify the goals and values of the society? Just what are such goals and values? Did the Hutchins Commission know exactly what these ideals were? There is obviously a wide diversity of social goals and values. Why should the press have to present and clarify them?

5. What is meant by "full access to the day's intelligence"? Does that mean that media have to tell everything? Just how much is enough for the Commission? Does it mean that *every* medium has such a responsibility, or that *all media together* have that responsibility? If the Commission means the latter, then is it assumed that every citizen be exposed to *all the media* so that they can get all the news?

Growing Media Ethical Sensitivity

In the years since the Hutchins Commission report, the American media have faced increasing criticism from individuals, groups, and government for their callousness, bias, unfairness, invasion of privacy, misrepresentations, and misplaced allegiances—all of which were mentioned in one way or another in the report. Journalists have long enjoyed bashing everything and everybody in sight; they are now beginning to get growing amounts of their own medicine.

Media people may well feel more important and powerful today than ever before. Celebrity journalism is common. Television political talk shows are giving journalists more public exposure. More and more media people are doing well on the lecture circuit. They are increasingly rubbing shoulders with the people who hold the seats of power and with the creative intellectuals. Historian Christopher Lasch (1995) proposes that journalism's ills are symptomatic of the arrogance pervading all professional elites. In an interview with Stephen Budiansky (1995, 47) Lasch states that as professionals are ever more removed from community ties and ordinary life, they develop a disdain for those they see as inferiors and manage to denigrate any genuine achievement or heroism. Budiansky quotes Lasch as saying that for the media "nothing is properly understood until it is exposed as corrupt, duplicitous or hypocritical."

As the media grow in power and as they cling to their "watchdog on government" role and other self-enhancing labels, they continue to indulge in what many people consider irresponsible or unethical practices. In their mad rush to meet deadlines and what they see as their prime responsibility "to let the people know," American journalists have long been pushing ethics into a small corner of their concern.

The journalistic love for constitutionally guaranteed press freedom has been a stimulant (or at least a defense) for many cases of questionable journalism. A few voices have, from time to time, warned journalists about carrying their freedom too far. One such voice is that of Walter Lippmann (1955, 97–100), who warned that the right of self-expression is "a private amenity rather than a public necessity." He noted further, echoing the spirit of the Hutchins Commission, that free expression has limits and that utterances should be true and significant. Lippmann proceeded to condemn unbridled freedom (which he called license) when it exploited the ignorance, and incited the passions, of the people. "Freedom" then, he wrote, "is such a hullabaloo of sophistry, propaganda, special pleading, lobbying, and salesmanship that it is difficult to remember why freedom of speech is worth the pain and trouble of defending it."

Toward a New Emphasis on Responsibility

Voices like Lippmann's seem to have set the stage for a growing concern. Journalists are bombarded from every side with ethical dilemmas, controversies, and questions and are hearing and reading more and more about their responsibilities. Some people have even suggested professionalizing journalism—having minimum entrance requirements, licenses, meaningful and forceful codes of ethics, and systems for removing recalcitrant and unethical practitioners. Ethics conferences abound, ombudsmen are increasing (albeit very slowly), critical press reviews (as in the *American Journalism Review*) note questionable media practices, and university courses in ethics proliferate. Despite this quantitative growth in concern, one may still wonder if the moral quality of the media is improving or if a monolithic concept of journalistic ethics is developing.

Many press people feel that talk of responsibility leads to obligations and duties and that these in turn tend to restrict press freedom. The journalists—especially those of the Enlightenment-libertarian persuasion—always get back to stressing *press freedom* and deemphasizing *press responsibility*. Perhaps what journalists should do is to recognize that press freedom can just as easily include the freedom to be positive as negative, and that it can include the freedom to be an ally or apologist for government as well as an adversary. In fact, when the press convinces itself that it is an adversary or watchdog on government, it restricts its own freedom by accepting a very limited role. This "adversary dogma," interestingly, is not even consistent with libertarian theory, and it would seem reasonable that journalists who talk about press freedom would not like being tied to this narrow role.

Communitarians, especially, fault the press for its negative and socially disruptive approach to news. Many journalists respond that the people want such an approach. How can journalists put their ethical "house" in order if they do not know that it is out of order? It appears that journalists, by and large, see themselves as a new breed of muckrakers, unearthing the unsavory aspects of society, the sensational and negative events. They also see themselves as a kind of permanent, relentless opposition to government. They must watch government carefully; they must protect the people from government excesses and crimes. At least, as the Hutchins Commission recommended, the media should try to give more reality to news coverage—good and bad, bright and dark, positive and negative, serious and entertaining. The media have the freedom as well as the responsibility to do this.

In many ways, the eighteenth-century French philosopher Jean-Jacques Rousseau was a forerunner of communitarianism, with its emphasis on social, rather than individual, concern. Freedom, for such thinkers, can be a dangerous thing and must be sacrificed to the social good. The philosopher Isaiah Berlin (1969, 189) clearly highlights Rousseau's relevance to the modern spirit of communitarianism: "Rousseau tells me that if I freely surrender all the parts of my life to society, I create an entity which, because it has been built by an equality of sacri-

21

fice to all its members, cannot wish to hurt any one of them; in such a society, we are informed, it can be nobody's interest to damage anyone else."

A Break with Tradition?

It is not easy for American journalists to be self-surrendering in Rousseauistic fashion. Tradition-bound libertarians that they are, most journalists do not want any kind of consensus ethics. In spite of their growing institutionalization and corporate awareness, they are largely suspicious of social ethics or any group-imposed rules that might cause them to lose their sense of identity and freedom. The press is, for the most part, so protective of the traditional ideas of individualism and pluralism that it resists anything that might result in standardization or conformity, even codes of ethics and news councils.

Evidence exists, however, that things are changing. Journalists may be starting to see ethics as the best policy for long-term success. Across the country, people are talking about the use of anonymous sources, inaccurate quotes, unbalanced stories, shocking and even gruesome photographs, gossip masquerading as news, political bias in the news, and a large number of other questionable practices.

Communitarians, as we have seen, desire a change away from the individualism of the past. Charles Derber (1993, 75) has written that "America is ripe for a communitarian awakening" and that "rugged individualism" has had its day. Increasingly, voices are heard repeating the kind of message that Margot Adler (1993, 77) of National Public Radio expresses: "Communitarians believe that Americans have become so focused on individual rights that they have forgotten that responsibilities go with them. . . . While they are few in number and more academic than activist, the communitarians see themselves as a new social movement that recommits America to a sense of shared responsibilities for the common good."

Although most journalists probably know little about communitarianism, they are becoming more conscious of their social or community responsibilities. Increasingly they are asking themselves: Do we print the name of the rape victim? What about the name of the accused rapist? Do we really believe in full-disclosure reporting—in the people's right to know? What are our real responsibilities and to whom are they owed? Do the ends (such as getting the story) really justify the means? Any means? Which means? Questions such as these, and many others, are currently being taken seriously by journalists.

The spirit of individualism, however, is certainly not gone. As Robert Bellah and his coauthors (1986, 142) have pointed out, "individualism lies at the very core of American culture." John Locke's individualism, they propose, is still very much alive in American thought, and the Lockean position that the individual "is prior to society, which comes into existence only through the voluntary contract of individuals . . . trying to maximize their own self-interest" is still influential (143). But Bellah and his colleagues warn that individualism, if not wisely harnessed by a sense of community, can be quite destructive and can lead to a kind of relative and incohesive morality.

Despite some obvious instances of unethical activities, undoubtedly spawned from time to time by the runaway individualism of specific journalists, the press seems to have received a message: It needs to be responsible. It needs to care more about ethics. The question now is whether journalists will put their awareness into action, whether they will move from the discussion level of ethical awareness to the everyday habitual level of actually "doing" ethics.

The cynic may still say that "an ethical press" is an oxymoron. But there is evidence that journalists are trying to remedy their excesses and moral lapses and to warrant public trust. For a long time, the press has unabashedly pummeled the weak-nesses of others and has set itself up as a paragon of virtue based solely on its own self-appraisal. Those days are over. The press itself is in the spotlight now, prompting journalists to clean up their ethical houses before exposing the dirt in the houses of others.

ANALYZING ETHICAL ISSUES

1. Beyond the journalists' belief that there should be ethical journal-ism, why do *you* think an ethical press is needed? If such a press is needed, this means that the current press is not ethical. How is society damaged by an unethical press? How can an audience member ascertain whether or not a newspaper, for example, is unethical? If the audience member doesn't know, then what differ-ence does it make if the newspaper does engage in unethical practices?

2. Can you describe any unethical practices in the news media of your city or area that have caused some type of harm to the prog-ress, health, or stability of your community? Are there so-called ethical practices that have also caused harm? When a news me-dium causes personal or social problems, should such journalistic practices be considered unethical? Why or why not?

3. If the society is basically unethical, and if the news media reflect this moral situation by being unethical themselves, what is wrong? Shouldn't the media reflect social reality? Can an ethical media system really be expected in an unethical social situation? How far ahead of their audiences should media be in the area of morality?

4. The communitarians say the liberal legacy of individualism and editorial autonomy is outdated. Do you think such an argument is valid? What would be the nature of communitarian reforms of journalism? Assuming that such reforms would somehow restrict or limit press freedom, what difference would that make? Why

Needed: A More Ethical Press

should press freedom be valued more than a harmonious, cooperative, and progressive society?

5. Do you think the Hutchins Commission gave impetus to the rise
of journalistic communitarianism? How would you compare the
Commission's concepts of social responsibility with those of the
communitarians? Both groups deprecate press-centered journalism in favor of society-centered journalism. How would socially
concerned journalism relate to agenda-setting? What would be the
impact on journalistic pluralism if communitarianism were to take
the place of libertarianism? Would such a changed journalism be a
good thing or a bad thing? Discuss.

References

Bellah, Robert N., et al. *Habits of the Heart: Individualism and Commitment
in American Life.* New York: Harper & Row (Perennial Library), 1986.
Berlin, Isaiah. *Four Essays on Liberty.* London: Oxford University Press,
1969.
Bogart, Leo. "Media and Democracy." *Media Studies Journal* (summer 1995).
Budiansky, Stephen. "The Media's Message." *U.S. News & World Report,* 9
January 1995.
Derber, Charles. "About Communitarians." *The Responsive Community* (fall
1993).
Hayakawa, S. I., and Alan R. Hayakawa. "The Empty Eye." *ETC.* (summer
1993).
Heiser, James. "C. S. Lewis As Media Critic." *The Intercollegiate Review*
(spring 1992).
Henry, William A., III. "When Reporters Break the Rules." *Time,* 15 March
1993.
Holmes, Stephen. *The Anatomy of Antiliberalism.* Cambridge: Harvard Uni-
versity Press, 1993.
Hughes, Frank. *Prejudice and the Press.* New York: Devin-Adair, 1950.
Hutchins Commission (Commission on Freedom of the Press). *A Free and
Responsible Press.* Chicago: University of Chicago Press, 1947.
Kurtz, Howard. "Why the Press Is Always Right." *Columbia Journalism Re-
view* (May–June 1993).
Lambeth, Edmund. *Committed Journalism.* Bloomington: Indiana University
Press, 1992.

Lasch, Christopher. *The Revolt of the Elites and the Betrayal of Democracy.* New York: Norton, 1995.

Lehrer, Jim. "Journalistic Arrogance." *Media Ethics Update,* vol. 6, no. 1 (fall 1993).

Lippmann, Walter. *Public Philosophy.* New York: Mentor Books, 1955.

Merrill, John C. *Legacy of Wisdom: Great Thinkers and Journalism.* Ames: Iowa State University Press, 1994.

Neiman Foundation. "Ethics on Trial: Tabloid Trash and Flash Threaten to Corrupt the American Media." *Nieman Reports,* vol. 48, no. 1 (spring 1994).

O'Neill, Michael J. *The Roar of the Crowd: How Television and People Power Are Changing the World.* New York: Times Books, 1993.

Quindlen, Anna. "The Media: Out of Control?—A Freewheeling Exchange on the Intrusive, Prurient, Run-amok (but More Democratic) Press." *New York Times Magazine,* 26 June 1994.

Robinson, Michael, and Norman Ornstein. "Why Press Credibility Is Going Down (and What to Do about It)." *Washington Journalism Review* (January–February 1990).

Safire, William. "Bringing Down the Nation's Public People." The *Columbia Missourian,* 30 May 1994.

Sandel, Michael J., ed. *Liberalism and Its Critics.* New York: New York University Press, 1984.

Self, Charles. "A Study of News Credibility." *International Communication Bulletin,* vol. 23, nos. 1–2 (spring 1988).

Siebert, Fred, Theodore Peterson, and Wilbur Schramm. *Four Theories of the Press.* Urbana: University of Illinois Press, 1956.

Smith, Ted J. "Are We Betraying the Public Trust?" *Communicator* (December 1992).

Tucher, Andie, and Dan Bischoff. "Scorned in an Era of Triumphant Democracy." *Media Studies Journal* (summer 1995).

Weaver, Paul H. *News and the Culture of Lying.* New York: Free Press, 1994.

CHAPTER TWO

THE DESIRE TO BE RESPONSIBLE

With the need for a more ethical or responsible journalism established in the preceding chapter, let us look now at the first step in achieving it. Journalists must want to be ethical. They may not always know exactly what is the right (or best) thing to do, but they can have ethical action as their objective. Journalists know that most audiences want responsible journalism; most also know that self-respect is important and that a sense of satisfaction comes from acting ethically. A journalist may be a communitarian, putting society or the group as paramount, or a journalist may be a libertarian, putting self-development and personal moral growth as the first priority. Either way, a journalist needs a will to be ethical. This is the starting point, this desire to be ethical, and without it journalists and their journalism will not improve.

Any person studying ethics learns very quickly that answers don't come easily, that many concepts are fuzzy, and that there is considerable disagreement even among writers and teachers about ethical theory (and practice). However, the important common denominator in all ethical discussion is *the attitude* of the person thinking about ethics.

What this attitude includes, of course, is a *desire to be responsible*, a deep-seated consciousness that doing the right

27

or best thing is better than simply doing something. A journalist, for instance, should be motivated by some underlying standard that prompts his or her daily work, regardless of the type of journalism being produced. A journalist must *care* about doing the right thing, must *want* to be ethical; such a sincere desire will lead the journalist to seek out moral wisdom as a guide to ethical decision making.

Stages of Ethical Development

Philosophers and psychologists tell us that we develop ethically through various stages. As we proceed through the stages, we are evidencing greater ethical maturity and sophistication. The Chinese philosopher T. H. Fang (1899–1977) suggested that one's nature develops into ethical "layers," each higher one fortifying the lower ones. Fang (1995, 508) lists these stages or layers, from lowest to highest, as follows: *homo faber* (craftsman), to *homo creator* (creator), to *homo sapiens* (person with knowledge), to *homo symbolicus* (symbolic or communicating person), to *homo honaestatis* (moral person), to *homo religiosus* (religious person). According to Fang, a person can develop from a lower to a higher level, or can regress to a lower level from a higher level.

Harvard psychologist Lawrence Kohlberg says that most people go through seven ethical stages. These range from the very lowest (fear of authority), through several intermediary stages, including hope of reward, peer approval, following the law, social utility, and duty to rules thought just. Finally, there is the highest, most autonomous ethical stage, that of being an ideal person, a person of principle.

How a person goes from one stage to another, from the lowest to the highest, depends on the person's desire to be ethical. Other factors enter the picture, but individual will is vitally important. In giving Kohlberg's central ethical idea,

Duska and Whelan (1995, 69) write that to "be one's own person . . . to mature fully" one must develop principles of judgment and action. Kohlberg himself (1971, 415) describes his highest level—the "post-conventional, autonomous, or principled level"—as one where there is the effort "to define moral values and principles which have validity and application apart from the authority of groups or persons holding these principles and apart from the individual's own identification with these groups."

The Danish philosopher Søren Kierkegaard (1813–1855) devised one of the earliest ethical progression models. He believed that a person's personal growth in ethics relates to the decisions one makes. This is a reflection of Kierkegaard's existentialist orientation. The most elemental level he called the *aesthetic* stage (pre-rational, youthful, restless), which is dominated by self-love and by spontaneous likes and dislikes. Kierkegaard's second (and higher) stage he termed the *ethical* (rational) stage, at which life acquires unity and coherence and the person is concerned with social obligations and fulfilling public expectations. Many people remain stuck in this stage, but some find it too formalistic and cold, too concerned with the *reasons* for doing this or that. Consequently, many people progress to the third and final stage—the highest one for Kierkegaard— the stage of *faith.*

Kierkegaard's stage of faith is a kind of religious stage, of beliefs, feelings, intuition, and emotion. It is similar to his first stage in its nonrational emphasis, but instead of being *self-centered*, it is *God-centered*. In coming to this last stage, people realize their personal inadequacies and see that reason has failed to bring contentment, so they finally find themselves in the Absolute (understood as God). We can see that Kierkegaard's highest ethical stage (unlike that of Kohlberg, which enthrones ethical autonomy) relinquishes rationality in morality and places supreme faith in intuition and transcendental sensitivity. This highest stage is quite similar to Fang's religious (*religiosus*) "layer."

Whether we are passing through the stages of Fang, Kohlberg, or Kierkegaard, the underlying motivation remains the same: the desire to be ethical. We may be ethical for the purpose of pleasing ourselves, an authority, our peers, or God, but the impetus is the will, or desire.

Wherever we may be on our ethical journey, we must determine to push on, to seek higher ground, if we desire to be ethical. James Fitzjames Stephen, a nineteenth-century British jurist and philosopher and a contemporary of John Stuart Mill, has expressed the importance of personal existential commitment that lies behind an ethical desire:

> Each must act as he thinks best, and if he is wrong so much the worse for him. We stand on a mountain pass in the midst of whirling snow and blinding mist, through which we get glimpses now and then of paths which may be deceptive. If we stand still, we shall be frozen to death. If we take the wrong road, we shall be dashed to pieces. We do not certainly know whether there is any right one. What must we do? "Be strong and of good courage." Act for the best, hope for the best, and take what comes (Warner, 1993, 212–13).

Foundational Ethical Questions

These words of Stephen are noble, indeed. But two basic questions probably should be asked at this point: Why should we even be concerned about ethics, about doing the right thing? And a collateral question: How do we know what is the right thing to do? These two questions are a foundation for any discussion of journalistic ethics—or *any* ethics, for that matter.

How can we answer them? First, journalists should be concerned about their ethics *because people in general are concerned.* The people for whom the journalists are working—

their publics—have expectations regarding the kind of journalism they get. And generally, people want journalism that is ethical. In other words, they want journalism that is dependable, credible, truthful, balanced, unbiased, thoughtful, interpretive, considerate, empathic, and realistic. We admit that these qualities may be difficult to achieve and that others, equally as virtuous, could be added. The point, however, is that there are audience expectations of journalism—expectations that should prompt journalists to take seriously the ethical dimensions of their work.

Audience concern with ethics is indeed an important reason for journalists to be ethical. But there is another reason, and it is just as important: Journalists should be ethical because they need *self-respect* and the sense of satisfaction that comes with *doing what one thinks is right*. Journalists have to live with themselves as well as with other people. In order to have meaningful lives, they need a sense of personal propriety, of integrity, and of self-esteem. To accomplish this, they must be concerned with trying to do the right thing, live up to their potential, and develop themselves beyond the materialistic aspects of their lives.

This emphasis on self-development, self-respect, and habitually striving for virtue has been stressed from the time of Aristotle to the present day (see box, p. 32). What is important to the individual-development ethicists is that a person be constantly striving to live a good moral life. A journalist, for instance, should concentrate on self-improvement and on practicing personal ethics. The Indian leader Mahatma Gandhi emphasized that a person's good habits are the key to an ethical life, and that one cannot really reform society or others without first being reformed from within one's self (Datta, 1953, 84). Gandhi gave prime attention to individualism in ethics. But he believed that self-reform could only be achieved by considering and including the interests of others (75).

Aristotle (384–322 B.C.)

Journalists wanting self-enhancement and maximum freedom used ethically will certainly wish to consider the philosophy of Aristotle, the famous Greek philosopher. A down-to-earth thinker who emphasizes the positive and presents a full vision of a virtuous and happy person, Aristotle stresses personal development, habitual good manners, and an appreciation of self-worth and personal happiness.

He would also tell journalists: Be wary of egalitarian and collectivistic philosophies; prize individual virtue and self-esteem; and be moderate in all things. In his great treatise, *The Nicomachean Ethics*, he presents his concept of the golden mean, which shows great concern for proper balance, for moderation. He proposes that ethical or right behavior is the balance or "mean" between thinking and acting in extreme ways. Moral excellence is a rough midpoint or mean between two kinds of badness—one of excess and the other of defect.

As flexible as Aristotle seems to be in his ethics, he is not a situationist. He calls some actions and thoughts absolutely bad and never even relatively desirable. For example, when it comes to murder, adultery, theft, envy, or malice, there is no golden mean; these are evil or unethical in themselves and should be avoided. But Aristotle is no Kant. He is more relativistic (or individu-

Ethics: A Basic Duality

This brings us to the duality of emphasis in journalistic ethics, which we introduced in the first chapter. It is important to recognize that the emphases of communitarians and libertari-

continued

alistic) and ties his ethics generally to seeking the golden mean.

Some of the extremes constantly face journalists and need to be reconciled with the golden mean. These include excessive vs. skimpy description; invading privacy vs. overcautious observing and questioning; insensitive pictures of accidents vs. avoidance of realism in pictures; overzealous accuracy in quotes vs. frequent and liberal tampering with quotes. For Aristotle, such cases would not be either/or situations but rather a search for the proper balance.

Aristotle has great respect for the individual and would have each journalist seeking self-fulfillment and achieving personal happiness. A rational pride in oneself and in one's moral character is good, according to Aristotle. The virtuous person relies on intelligence as a guide. The modern journalist who respects reason, the scientific approach, objectivity, absolutes, self-fulfillment, and personal happiness will find a friend in Aristotle, who saw no limits on the human spirit. It is, perhaps, easier for some journalists to admire Plato, with his social consciousness and his reforming zeal. But it is good for the world to have had the calm rationalism and individualism of Aristotle to balance the flamboyant idealism and communitarianism of Plato.

ans are not mutually exclusive. The communitarians put the society or community development and harmony first, while the libertarians put the individual and personal ethics and self-development first (see Figure 2-1).

C. S. Lewis (1943, 7) points out the need to be concerned

FIGURE 2-1
TWO ETHICAL MEGA-EMPHASES

LIBERTARIANISM

Enlightenment Liberals
Individualism
Diversity
Competition
Existentialism
Pluralistic society
Meritocracy
Maximum freedom of expression
Relative/pragmatic ethics

Personal ethical codes
Personal transformation
"Inner-directed" motivation
Self-enhancement
Self-reliance
Anti-media professionalization
Full-spectrum news

COMMUNITARIANISM

Groupists/Cooperationists
Networking/social cohesion
Conformity/bonding
Cooperation
Absolutism
Universal solidarity
Egalitarianism
Restrained freedom
Absolute/normative/universal
ethics
Legalistic ethical codes
"Civic transformation"
"Other-directed" motivation
Selflessness
Like-minded worldview
Media professionalization
"Positive"/"Socially helpful"
news

EXEMPLARS
Lao-Tsu, Socrates, Aquinas,
Milton, Locke, Hume, Voltaire,
Constant, Jefferson, Mill,
Nietzsche, Thoreau, Camus,
Jaspers, Rand, Nozick

EXEMPLARS
Confucius, Plato, Augustine,
Rousseau, Hegel, Marx,
Niebuhr, Hutchins, Bellah,
MacIntyre, Lasch, Sandel,
Jonas, Etzioni, Rawls

with *both* the social and the individual aspects of morality. He writes that morality is concerned "with fair play and harmony between individuals," but that it also must be dedicated to "tidying up or harmonising the things inside each individual." Furthermore, he warns that unless we go beyond the first aspect and get to the second—the tidying up inside each human being—we "are only deceiving ourselves" (72). It would seem that one emphasis without the other would have little meaning for any journalist who was trying to be ethical. Thus, both approaches will be introduced here. Let us look first at the "social ethics" emphasis.

Social or Communitarian Ethics

We have seen that audience expectations provide one reason for the journalist's desire to be ethical. This concern leads naturally to the field of social or communitarian ethics, in which the emphasis is on the group, the society. What should we as journalists do to benefit others? What should we do that will bring happiness or other benefits—material, spiritual, emotional, or psychological—to those around us? Bringing benefits to others is a noble reason for being ethical, and it certainly draws many young people into journalism. This was the emphasis of Plato (see box, p. 36), Rousseau, and J. S. Mill in earlier times, and more recently of sociologist Amitai Etzioni and philosophers John Rawls and Alasdair MacIntyre.

Where did communitarianism start? Perhaps it was Plato himself in ancient Greece who gave birth to the philosophy of communitarian ethics. He urged people (in *The Laws, Book 12*) to act in concert, never independently, to advance together toward the same goals, and to always have a common way of life. Plato's admonition was echoed in the eighteenth century by German philosopher Georg Hegel, who proposed a morality based not on individual reasoning or personal conscience but

Plato (427–347 B.C.)

The Greek philosopher Plato's dialogs, in which philosophers such as Socrates talk about justice and other concepts, give insights into Plato's thinking. Today, journalists who wish to understand the nature of objective journalism and to glean political insights will find these Platonic dialogs of great value. *The Republic* is perhaps Plato's best-known work; it sheds light on the kind of stratified social structure he would recommend.

Plato might be called one of the forefathers of communitarianism. He sees individuals joining with others harmoniously as the main standard of value—the "community as a whole," with each person sacrificing individuality and merging into the aggregate or collective. According to Plato, the omnipotent state follows naturally, and the authority of the state must be unlimited. Government must provide parental care for the people: It must educate, censor all literature and art, assign all persons to their jobs, and regulate economic activities.

Journalists, then, would merge into the group and fulfill duties contributing to the progress and stability of the employing mass medium. The mass medium itself would be at the service of the state. Journalists would not rock the social boat but would cooperate with the social

on following social custom, on giving up individuality in ethics and living a life of concrete social duties. Hegel said, in effect, that a person who submits to the state or to a group, while losing much personal freedom, is gaining a higher freedom. This idea had a profound impact on Marx and Hitler, each of whom adapted the concept to his particular brand of socialism.

The Chinese philosopher Hsun Tzu (ca. 340–245 B.C.)

continued

engineering. In Plato's view, morality would be defined by "philosopher kings," and ethical journalists would simply do the will of the authorities. Plato's ethics would be a kind of statist utilitarianism, in which the criterion of morality is the interest of the state.

Plato talked of cardinal virtues, and these might be helpful to journalists: *wisdom,* the intellectual base for ethics; *courage,* helping one pursue goals that wisdom has set; *temperance,* which urges moderation and gives harmony to the moral life; and finally, *justice,* which involves a person's deservedness. This final virtue does not mean equal treatment. Rather, in today's world, it might mean that some public officials would receive more attention on television than others—if they deserved it.

Platonists put social good ahead of personal freedom. Likewise, they would place press responsibility above the concept of press freedom. Many journalists—kindred spirits of the Hutchins Commission of the 1940s—would find this acceptable. Others would find it dangerous. Plato's complexity permits various interpretations of his stimulating ideas, and this brief profile gives only a hint of his philosophical views.

presented a very early communitarian view. Hsun Tzu believed that people are by nature selfish, and he took a position quite like that of Plato, who believed that benevolence and righteousness do not spring from human nature but must be formed by government, law, and community conventions. Hsun Tzu emphasized education, believing it would "cultivate" goodness in people. According to Hsun Tzu, it is through moral discipline and pressure by the community that people learn to change their natures and become good.

Another representative of early communitarianism was the Chinese philosopher Han Fei, a pupil of Hsun Tzu. Han Fei also believed that human nature was rebellious and evil and— like Plato and Rousseau in the West—that the state or the community should always be put before the individual. He was devoted to regimentation for the good of society. Like Machiavelli, Han Fei advised rulers on how to advance their positions, consolidate their strength, and protect society from any doctrine or practice that might harm the power of the state.

Communitarians today still desire social order as much as did Plato or Hegel, or Hsun Tzu or Han Fei, but they reject any suggestion that they are authoritarian or tyrannical. They are concerned with social stability, but they insist that they are also champions of liberty. Communitarians hope that education, a high moral consciousness, and peer pressure (with some laws, of course) will bring individuals into a harmonious and cooperating "community."

Amitai Etzioni (1993) points to a civil society in disarray and offers a communitarian solution, especially to the professional middle class of Americans. He believes that social agreement has yielded to unbridled self-aggrandizement and the ethos of instant gratification. Etzioni recommends a momentous cultural shift away from individualism and toward a new concern for others.

Emphasizing the Community

The communitarian or group-oriented ethicist is one who sublimates personal ethical values to societal desires and expectations. Or, said another way, the communitarian would have individuals form their ethical standards by looking at their group's expectations. Communitarians are suspicious of pluralistic or individualistic ethics—of libertarianism in ethical decision making. There is an underlying doubt about the rationality and moral sense of the average person. The communitarian ethicists want a community-based ethics, a more monolithic, common concept of morality. They share, to various degrees, a suspicion of Enlightenment concepts such as individualism and freedom, which have been espoused by such philosophers as Locke, Voltaire, Kant, and J. S. Mill. They see Enlightenment concepts as outmoded, as leading to a competitive and selfish morality that endangers any kind of community cohesion and development.

Contending that they do not depreciate the individual or offer an invitation to the safe haven of collectivism, communitarians say they simply wish to stress that ethics is *relational*, concerned with interactions and connections. Many communitarians do, however, seem to opt for a more absolute or universal kind of ethics, largely established by the wishes of the community, and they are not averse to the idea of using social pressures to bring the individual in line with such majoritarian-determined ethics. Beyond that, they are rather vague as to how they might "enforce" their social ethics. They say that the concern for being ethical drives ethics and that moral dialog and education can facilitate a more monolithic ethics through the communication of social mores and expectations.

The Communitarian Journalist

Clifford Christians of the University of Illinois has been in the vanguard of communitarian ethics within the academic community. In a 1993 book, he fills in some of the details of communitarian journalism. He would have journalists throw out the liberal politics of rights, which he believes "rests on unsupportable foundations" (45). According to Christians, these rights (such as journalistic autonomy) should be "given up for a politics of the common good."

From the communitarian perspective, journalists should ask such questions as What do *we* want? or What do *you* want? rather than What do *I* want? Communitarian journalists would discard the old concepts of journalistic self-determination, individualism, and "negative" (nonactive) freedom. Instead of stressing "freedom from" outside controls, they would opt for "positive" freedom, with its emphasis on doing *something positive* for society (Christians, 42–44). Also, they would have news stories be accurate, balanced, relevant, and complete (55), an idea reminiscent of the Hutchins Commission report discussed earlier. Few conscientious reporters would quibble with this as an abstract goal, but the problem comes in determining the precise definition of accuracy, the factors comprising balance, the focus of relevance (relevant to what?), and the degree of completeness necessary. Like the Hutchins Commissioners, the communitarians are not forthcoming with answers.

Morality "always makes universal and categorical claims," according to Christians and his coauthors (61). There are "nonnegotiable principles," they say, such as truth-telling and the public's right to know (55). Perhaps a primary communitarian tenet is that journalists should realize that "universal solidarity is the normative core of the social and moral order" (14). This would require that there be some kind of group-dictated ethical standards to guide journalism. It would also underscore one of the communitarians' basic beliefs: that journalists must reject "the Enlightenment's individualistic rationalism" (185).

In summary, the ethical emphasis of the communitarians would have the media: (1) publish those things that would bring people together, not fractionalize them; (2) give the people of the community what they desire, not what the journalists want them to have; (3) refrain from publishing anything that would tear down community spirit; (4) agree on a common ethics; and (5) refrain from falling into the trap of embracing situational or relativistic ethics.

The Desire to Be Responsible

Personal or Individual Ethics

The second reason for being concerned with ethics—the self-enhancement reason we mentioned earlier in this chapter—leads us into the area of *personal* or *individual* ethics. The emphasis here is on the development of one's self, on self-discipline, and on the self-determination to rise to higher moral levels. The individual is ever seeking to perform habitual *right actions*, which are based primarily on personally determined virtues. The key to personal ethics comes down to *self-respect*, to developing one's character in the Aristotelian sense: having a structure of life examined by ourselves as if we were our own spectators.

Let us look a moment at the Scottish philosopher David Hume (1711–1776). He believed that individuals need a sense of personhood and pride in order to make them cognizant of their own merit and give them confidence. Hume considered self-respect "the crowning attitude" for a person trying to live a moral life; such a person, for Hume, was a "descendant of Aristotle's great-souled man" (Hudson, 1986, 64). Like Aristotle, Hume's ethical focus was on the development of character, on personal dedication to habitual allegiance to virtues. Hume obviously recognized the importance of human interaction within groups and communities (the *polis*), but what was foremost was personal moral development—the individual structuring of "character." In this sense, David Hume exemplifies the dominant thrust of the individualist spirit.

The theologian Reinhold Niebuhr, although a member of the Hutchins Commission and surely a proponent of media responsibility, recognized that the community itself could foster conformism, and he saw this as bad. He wrote (1957, xix) that the community can become "the arbiter of opinion," making nonconformity difficult by "the weight of standardized opinion." Thus, he noted, "the community becomes the tyrant through the conception of itself projected by the images of the mass media." Certainly no David Hume in his belief in individualism, Niebuhr at least recognized the weakness of community-based values spread through the mass media.

Developing Internal Standards

The individual ethicist insists that ethics is self-determined, voluntary conduct; it has to do with self-legislation and self-enforcement. While recognizing that ethics must operate in society and in relation to others, the individual ethicist places the burden of responsibility on the person—not on the community, the society, or on others. Such a position is tied very closely to *existentialism*, a philosophy in which personal self-formation is paramount, freedom of individual action is served, and individual responsibility is required.

It is quite true, as communitarians insist, that the individualist mode of ethics opens the door for contradictory actions, for fractionalizing society, and for decisions that may harm social progress toward specific goals. It can lead to a contentiousness, a relativism, and kind of competitiveness in the field of ethics, all of which can be frustrating to those seeking social harmony.

Stephen Holmes (1993) is not sympathetic to the communitarian perspective. According to Holmes, communitarian critics of liberalism assume that because, in a liberal society, no particular moral code has official status, liberalism abandons all moral principles. This, he points out, is not true. The liberal simply puts the development of moral principles in the hands of the individual. Also, says Holmes, communitarian critiques of liberal individualism assume that individualism is antisocial, whereas it actually involves a heightened concern for others, as individuals rather than just as group members.

Communitarian critics of liberal individualism tend to see journalists as separate, free-spirited, existential persons who impede any kind of social solidarity in ethical thinking. To the communitarian, such journalists are antisocial persons, running in all directions, doing their own things, without any discipline or concern for the team or the spectators. This concept of journalism as individualism gone wild—a kind of autonomous ethical nihilism or antigroup functioning—is a gross distortion, say the liberal descendants of the Enlightenment.

Suspicion of Group-Mindedness

In another book (Merrill, 1989), I have maintained that journalists tend to gravitate toward a kind of group-oriented ethics and find the individual ethical approach somewhat traumatic. Individualists certainly do not endorse such a trend, but they recognize its pull. The following quote presents this view: "The average news operation disdains individualism. The person with integrity, a sense of self-respect, and a love for individuality is seen as a threat to the organization. This type of journalist is looked upon increasingly as a 'poor team player,' one who does not fit nicely into the system of corporate journalism. In short, the mode of personal freedom is not a very popular or profitable one" (123).

Another modern individualist, magazine journalist Lewis H. Lapham (1973), bemoans a kind of deep-seated desire among press people to belong to a group, organization, or profession. He notices in the press more and more talk about "legitimate" journalists, implying a willingness to accept some type of licensing or certification so that, presumably, *bona fide* journalists can be identified.

Lapham writes that the more the press becomes a profession, the more it will "discourage the membership of rowdy amateurs" and, as it is with other professions, "encourage the promotion of people diligently second-rate" (32). It does seem that there is, among many journalists, a basic desire to belong to an exclusive group, to have some kind of special status that will stimulate them to be more skilled and perhaps even more ethical.

Despite this strong pull toward organizational, community, or social conformity, the personal or individualist appeal of Enlightenment thinking (with its resonation into the romanticism of the nineteenth century) continues to influence the modern journalist. Many feel uneasy with the communitarian's advocacy of group harmony, preferring to retain a substantial degree of contentiousness and individuality. This is not an easy position today, as journalism may sublimate the individual in the group effort. As one modern sociologist (Ellul, 1969, 221) notes, the individual "is drowned in the mass and becomes convinced that he is only a cipher."

The older libertarian or individualist emphasis in American journalism got its impetus from the European Age of Reason, primarily from the Enlightenment ideas in Britain and France. Europeans such as Voltaire, Locke, Milton, and John Stuart Mill and early Americans like Madison and Jefferson had faith in individual citizens and in their ability to make rational decisions. These liberals respected a free flow of information, pluralistically determined, and thought that a diversity of ideas and opinions was good for society, even though such diversity might be disruptive and contain many false or wrong-headed messages. These libertarian thinkers, repudiating the elitist and authoritarian ideas of previous times, had a healthy respect for all kinds of opinions and rebelled against the notion of controlling what the people ought to know.

John Stuart Mill, for example, was a staunch libertarian (see his *On Liberty*) who was critical of society gaining more power over the individual. He believed people could improve themselves by cultivating individuality, and he bemoaned the growth of conformity, which tended to diminish self-awareness and damage social progress. For him, conformity was largely promoted through education, communication, and commercial interests. Typical of the inheritors of the eighteenth-century

Enlightenment, Mill considered reason and individual liberty to be of paramount importance. Mill's ideas about freedom can be capsulized in these words: that a person should be free to express any opinions—in speech, in writing, and in behavior—as long as that person does not interfere with someone else's freedom.

Existentialism: Two Voices

During the nineteenth century and the first half of the twentieth century, another intellectual movement added its emphasis on the individual and on freedom to that of the Enlightenment. This philosophy was Existentialism, which had its main impact on the continent of Europe but also made considerable inroads in the Americas. Existentialism is a philosophy of subjectivism, individualism, commitment, action, and personal responsibility. It espouses personal development as a prelude to social development. It seeks authentic existence and is dedicated to a sense of personal integrity. It extols taking chances, experimenting, and making personal choices.

Existentialists rebel against being pigeonholed or subsumed by a group and being "common" cogs in the machinery of a community. They would certainly embrace a personal ethics, one that springs from internal sources and is not imposed by the social pressures of peer groups. Existentialists clearly show that individualistic ethics is not tied to "negative freedom," as the communitarians claim; they give great emphasis to using freedom actively and positively. In short, they insist on doing something with their freedom; it is only by this action that they "make themselves," that they create their essence from their existence. If they did not act, if they were stuck in the mode of negative freedom (having no outside controls on them), they would be inauthentic and, in fact, nothing more than stones.

Kierkegaard One very early existentialist voice, in the 1800s, was Søren Kierkegaard. This Danish philosopher, often considered the founder of modern existentialism, rebelled against socially directed morality and urged individualism and personal freedom. For him, being subsumed by a group, the state, or the community was a rejection of a person's status as a "genuine human being" as "the cowardly denial of one's true selfhood" (Mullen, 1981, 48). Kierkegaard stressed living and seeking satisfaction and fulfillment as an individual, rather than following the other path of living through the group.

Kierkegaardian individualism, in the modern world, is being increasingly depreciated, as organizations, groups, communities, and society as a whole become the focal points of a complex global network. Philosopher Karl Jaspers (1957, 51) summed up the trend toward groupism by noting that the average person has "no more genuine individuality than one pin in a row, a mere object of general utility." Jaspers goes on to say that society is becoming more and more "an apparatus," a collective sense of cooperation and harmony that enthrones social stability and minimizes individual initiative (51–52). This social apparatus, says Jaspers, smothers the individual, who increasingly is "regarded with indifference."

Nietzsche Another existentialist, Friedrich Nietzsche (1844–1900), who came on the European scene a decade or so after Kierkegaard, reinforced the Dane's individualistic philosophy and built on his existentialism. Nietzsche called for the personal creation of values and the enthroning of authenticity. His instruction to "Become the person you are" is the underlying principle of his moral theory. One must beware of taking values from the majority, Nietzsche warns, a practice that degrades the self and reduces one to being simply a member of "a herd" (Shutte, 1984, 105–106).

Nietzsche was recommending a transvaluation of all values, acknowledging that a person's individuality—if it is "life-enhancing"—may well cause some disruption of social harmony and even threaten political authority (Shutte, 175). Many ethicists today probably would find Nietzsche's concepts too individualistic and nonconformist, seeing them as a danger to the growth of the communitarian spirit. For the conservative or traditional ethicist, Nietzsche's ideas seem to foster egocentric, even eccentric, activities and split apart the social fabric. A more accurate interpretation of Nietzsche, however, might consider him as more than an individualist. For Nietzsche saw the person not as some atom departed from society but as a self-valuing individual who develops a constantly improving self that transcends social pressures and does not fall prey to them. Such an "Overman"—or superior person—impacts society in a primary way, rather than being impacted by society. Regardless of how one interprets Nietzsche, it is safe to say that he comes down on the side of the individualistic ethicist, rather than on the side of the communitarian or socially directed one.

The Collateral Question

Let us now return to the collateral question posed early in this chapter: How do I know what is the right thing to do? This is the foundational question to a normative ethics, and we cannot really answer it. This whole book is an attempt to answer it, but it falls short, as all attempts do. There are many theories of normative ethics, of ethics that tell us what to do. These theories will be dealt with in more depth in the next chapter, but at this point the question can be touched on briefly.

Tied in with normative ethics are the reasons for doing one thing versus another. And when we start providing *reasons* for ethical action, we are solidly into *rational* ethics. You may be asking, Is there any other kind? Yes. Many ethicists through the ages have suggested that there are nonrational manifestations (spiritual, metaphysical, transcendental, instinctive, emotive, or inspirational) of what are the proper or right actions. For these, persons cannot give reasons for their ethical deci-

47

sions; they can only say that they "feel" or "intuit" what is the proper thing to do.

Rational Considerations

We can determine what to do rationally, and there are various ways to do this (for example, by using reason to derive *a priori* guiding maxims or principles to follow, or by using reason to weigh the production of good consequences). Or, we can rationally decide to synthesize these two ethical positions: We can have basic ethical principles but be willing to deviate from them when reason suggests a higher good in a specific situation.

In regard to how we know if we are doing the right thing, it should be said that quite often we *don't* know. We consider our moral rules, our alternative possibilities for action, our general values, our personal commitments and loyalties—and then we do the best we can. But we are never certain we have done the right thing, or at least never certain we have done the best thing. Ethics, we must remember, is not an exact science, and it never will be, even if society were to decide on an absolute or universal set of ethical standards. Such a normative code might be absolute or universal in its application, but there is no assurance it would be the most ethical or correct code.

Inborn Moral Sense

As we progress further into this book, the reader will realize that ethics has to do with a complex, sophisticated, and subjective array of possibilities, which are brought into consciousness by what seems to be a universal and deep-seated desire: the basic human desire to be ethical. Often this is referred to as a "moral sense" or a personal "conscience." It is something that does not tell us exactly what to do to be ethical, but it does give us clues and hints as to what our actions should be.

The Desire to Be Responsible

Probably the best recent discussion of this inborn moral sense is given by James Q. Wilson (1993, 25). He believes that such a sense in a person "emerges as naturally as his sense of beauty or ritual (with which morality has much in common) and that it will affect his behavior, though not always and in some cases not obviously." But, Wilson asks, how can one reconcile such a moral sense with the evidence of depravity, immoral oppression, and amoral self-indulgence that we see all around us? Here is his answer:

> The moral sense is no surer a cause of moral action than that beliefs are the cause of actions generally. Behavior is the product of our senses interacting with our circumstances. But when we behave in ways that seem to violate our fundamental moral sensibilities . . . we offer reasons, and the reasons are never simply that we enjoy such acts and think that we can get away with them. The justifications we supply invariably are based on other claims, higher goods, or deferred pleasures (25).

As we proceed into the next chapter, where we consider some of the main theories or concepts of ethics, we should recognize that our attitude toward ethics is most important, that our desire to be ethical is the real foundation of journalistic responsibility, and that our natural moral sense will at least alert us when we find ourselves skating on thin ethical ice. Just what we do about the various ethical conundrums that face us, and how we manage to cross the thin ice with our basic integrity intact, are the practical problems confronting every journalist who retains this basic desire to be ethical. Many journalists will fall through the ice and clamber out to skate again, readjusting their old theories to the needs of new environments. Other journalists, because of a lack of resolve, persistence, and effort, may not survive ethically and may drown in the icy waters of irresponsibility.

ANALYZING ETHICAL ISSUES

1. How do you feel about journalists who do not desire to be responsible or ethical? Should there be some kind of ethical sensitivity test given to them before they get a job at a news medium? Who should give such a test—the medium or a journalism education institution? Do you think such a test of ethical awareness/aspiration could be designed that would actually be meaningful and helpful?

2. How do you feel about ethical stages that people purportedly go through—for example, Kohlberg's seven stages? Might not a journalist actually *start* at the highest (autonomous) stage, desiring to be an ideal, principled person? How could Kierkegaard's three-stage progression model be adapted to a journalist who is *not* a religious person? Would not Kierkegaard's second stage (fulfilling social obligations) be for a journalist *a higher* ethical stage than his third stage (faith)?

3. In the world of pragmatic, competitive, and success-oriented American journalism, what would you give as some of the main reasons a journalist *would want* to be ethical? How would it "pay off" for the journalist? Could it possibly result in doing as good a story as could be done by playing fast and loose with ethics?

4. C. S. Lewis says that you cannot make a person good by law. Is this really true? Cannot law—or even hard-and-fast editorial principles—make journalists good? Or at least better? Is not a firm, well spelled-out editorial policy preferable to none at all—or to a pluralistic one?

5. Let us hypothesize that both the *libertarian* and the *communitarian* journalist desire to be ethical. One is motivated by personal desires, and the other by social desires. Which one do you think will do the right thing more often? Which one of these basic orientations best describes you at this time? Why?

The Desire to Be Responsible

References

Christians, Clifford, John Ferre, and Mark Fackler. *Good News: Social Ethics and the Press.* New York: Oxford University Press, 1993.

Datta, Dhirendra M. *The Philosophy of Mahatma Gandhi.* Madison: University of Wisconsin Press, 1953.

Duska, Ronald, and Mariellen Whelan. *Moral Development: A Guide to Piaget and Kohlberg.* New York: Paulist Press, 1995.

Ellul, Jacques. *Propaganda.* New York: Alfred Knopf, 1965.

Etzioni, Amitai. *The Spirit of Community: Rights, Responsibilities, and the Communitarian Agenda.* New York: Crown Publishers, 1993.

Fang, T. H. In *ROC Yearbook, 1995* ("Philosophy," 499–510).

Holmes, Stephen. *The Anatomy of Antiliberalism.* Cambridge: Harvard University Press, 1993.

Hudson, Stephen D. *Human Character and Morality.* London: Routledge & Kegan Paul, 1986.

Hutchins Commission (Commission on Freedom of the Press). *A Free and Responsible Press.* Chicago: University of Chicago Press, 1947.

Jaspers, Karl. *Man in the Modern Age.* New York: Anchor Books, 1957.

Kohlberg, Lawrence, and P. Turiel. "Moral Development and Moral Education." In *Psychology and Educational Practice*, edited by G. Lesser. Glenview, Il.: Scott, Foresman, 1971.

Lapham, Lewis. "Hierarchical Longing within the Press." *Harper's* (August 1973).

Lewis, C. S. *Mere Christianity.* New York: Macmillan, 1943.

Merrill, John C. *The Dialectic in Journalism: Toward a Responsible Use of Press Freedom.* Baton Rouge: Louisiana State University Press, 1989.

Mullen, John D. *Kierkegaard's Philosophy: Self-Deception and Cowardice in the Present Age.* New York: New American Library (Mentor Books), 1981.

Niebuhr, Reinhold. Introduction to *Responsibility in Mass Communication*, by Wilbur Schramm. New York: Harper & Brothers, 1957.

Shutte, Ofelia. *Beyond Nihilism: Nietzsche without Masks.* Chicago: University of Chicago Press, 1984.

Warner, Stuart D. (ed.). *Liberty, Equality, Fraternity*, by James Fitzjames Stephen. Indianapolis: Liberty Fund Press, 1993.

Wilson, James Q. *The Moral Sense.* New York: Free Press, 1993.

CHAPTER THREE

MAIN ETHICAL ROADS

Ethical roads, or theories, are many and varied, and journalists travel several of these roads. What is difficult for many to understand is that journalists can be ethical if they travel any one of them. Presumably, all roads lead to the same destination: ethical journalism. "I am not printing the rape victim's name," one journalist says. "I am being ethical." "I am definitely printing the rape victim's name," the other journalist says. "I am being ethical." They are both right. It would seem that the salient consideration is the motivation to be ethical, not the specific reasoning behind the action.

The two major emphases (libertarianism and communitarianism) discussed in the first two chapters do not explain much about the principal ethical roads (or theories) of ethics. They do, however, give some indication as to how different people will relate to ethics, which theories people are likely to adopt, and whether they will tend to endorse more or less freedom in journalism.

The communitarian journalist would seek more harmony and agreement in the practice of journalism; the libertarian would support more diversity and contention. The communitarian journalist would want to see more absolute or universal ethical norms and less social contention, while the libertarian journalist would support more flexible, relative, and personal ethics. And these proclivities do, indeed, relate to the various theories and subtheories of ethics dealt with in this chapter.

These two ethical orientations say little, however, about the actual normative ethical standards that might be used by journalists. For instance, the libertarian (individualistic) journalist can choose to be ethical through inner-direction, while the communitarian is more other-directed. It is simply that one orientation proceeds in ethics from the person to the group, and the other proceeds from the group to the person. The libertarian stresses self-enhancement that will improve society; the communitarian would enhance the community, thereby improving the individual as a part of it.

Another binary way of looking at broad ethical theories is by considering whether one gives primacy to *ethical acts* or to *ethical character* (the agent). Let us look at these two views briefly.

The Direct and Indirect Views of Ethics

The fact that there are two major ethical views has to do not so much with what specific things are ethical or unethical but rather with how we conceive of ethics in the first place. In other words, this binary perspective is part of the *metaethical* (more basic, theoretical) realm. The two concepts have been called the *direct* and the *indirect* views (Hudson, 1986). What makes a theory or view direct or indirect "is located in its conception of what morality is *about*" (8). In essence, the direct view holds that morality is principally about *acts* or *conduct;* they must be assessed as primary ethical phenomena, and this assessment is the main moral task. Other factors—motives, for instance—are seen as secondary and derivative. On the other hand, the indirect view denies the primacy of acts held by the direct view. It holds, instead, that the *moral agent* (human character) has equal standing with, or even superiority to, acts.

We see, then, that the direct and indirect views are broad philosophical descriptions of the nature of morality.

The direct view can subsume a number of different moral theories, some of which we deal with in this chapter; it can be found in utilitarian theory, modern Kantian theory, or in intuitionist theory. The basic moral question of the direct view is this: *What ought I do?* (The fundamental moral question in the indirect view is: *What kind of person ought I be?*) The direct view takes as "an obvious truism that acts have primacy, that the virtue of acts is the concern of morality" (Hudson, 5). This view is so common that many people accept it as the only description of the nature of moral theorizing. It is the orthodox view of morality, and very few philosophers (such as Aristotle and Hume) oppose it.

The second metaethical perspective is the indirect view. Whereas the direct view is concerned mainly with the assessment of acts or kinds of acts, the indirect view has a broader concern—the formation of moral character. Its basic questions are: *How should one live?* and *What kind of character should one develop?* The indirect view, characterized by Aristotle's "virtue ethics" and Confucius's "human-heartedness," holds that one cannot go directly to principles of conduct (deciding this is ethical and this is not). Instead, people must take indirect paths to arrive at principles. They must examine the nature of moral character—or moral *agency*—in order to answer the kinds of questions that the direct view considers basic. Let us move on now from these grand theoretical considerations to the more practical normative highways of ethical theory.

Entering the Theoretical Highways

Anyone studying ethics will note that authors place various ethical systems or theories in a number of different categories and that these are not always in agreement. There are probably as many labels given to ethical theories as there are people who discuss them. Here we shall subsume various ethical systems into two main ones, which will be called *pragmatic ethics* and *humanistic ethics*. This may appear to be an unusual typology, but I believe that it is a realistic one (see Figure 3-1).

What is called pragmatic ethics would, to many people, not be considered ethics at all. It is concerned with achieving ends, gaining success, and doing what one sets out to do. The main motivation is the desire for success, and the ends are generally more important than the means. The journalist subscribing to this form of ethics would, for example, want his or her reportorial tactics "to work," to achieve their primary objective of getting the best (most thorough and accurate) story possible. This journalist would use conventional practices, those that tend to conform with traditional ethical wisdom only if they would achieve the ends desired.

The other main category of ethical theories, here referred to as humanistic ethics, is what most of us think of simply as "ethics"—doing the right or best thing, not out of selfish motives but out of a desire to be more "humane," to consider the feelings and needs of others, and to bring more moral harmony to the society. Under this rubric, we will consider in this chapter the ethics of Immanuel Kant (*deontological*) and John Stuart Mill (*teleological*). We will also consider *personalist* ethics as a form of humanistic ethics. Personalist ethics is a more subjective, nonrational ethics comprising a wide assortment of subtheories, from religious ethics to existential ethics. Let us now look more closely at the first main theory, pragmatic ethics.

Pragmatic Ethics

This genre of journalistic ethics might well be considered a type of "professional ethics" in that journalists focus on the professional goal of providing the best story—letting "the peo-

FIGURE 3-1
ETHICAL HIGHWAYS AND BYWAYS

PRAGMATIC ETHICS
(Motivation: DESIRE FOR SUCCESS)
(Exemplar: MACHIAVELLI)

[Rational]

• Form of consequential (teleological) ethics
• Achieving predetermined, practical ends
• Ends more important than means

HUMANISTIC ETHICS
(Motivation: DESIRE FOR VIRTUE)

[Rational]

DEONTOLOGICAL (I. Kant)—legalistic,
a priori rules/maxims/duty to principle
(absolutist, universal)
TELEOLOGICAL (J. S. Mill)—consideration of
consequences (relative); greatest good to greatest
number or self

[Non-rational]

PERSONALIST (Kierkegaard)
• Subjective/instinctual/conscience (moral sense)/
sensitivity/situational/spiritual guidance, etc.
• Antinomian *ad hoc* ethics (relative)
• Situationist (e.g., J. Fletcher)—*agape-driven*
• Existential (subjective) ethics (Exemplars: Sartre, Camus, Nietzsche, Jaspers)

FIGURE 3-1
CONT.

Some Ethical Subtheories or Byways
Acquired-virtue (Aristotle)
Relativistic
Absolutist
Objectivist
Religious
Egoistic
Utilitarian
Intuitive
Social Contract
Existentialist
Social (Communitarian)
Individualist (Libertarian)
Machiavellian

Plus many roads of mixed or overlapping theories

---

ple know" to the fullest extent possible. If journalists have this kind of dedication, they will concentrate on being successful in this endeavor; providing forthright and full-disclosure stories will be the driving force of their journalism. (Of course, if journalists desire to fulfill other agenda, the driving force of their journalism may involve biasing, censoring, or otherwise tampering with stories. But such journalism would probably fall outside of ethics and reside in the field of propaganda or *egocentric pragmatics.*)

The pragmatic ethics we are referring to here is at least marginally in the field of ethics, because journalists are achieving success by letting people know the truth as fully as possible. In a way, they are altruistic, not egoistic. Journalists want to achieve a serious professional goal, and to do this they may on occasion

FIGURE 3-2
MACHIAVELLIAN ETHICS

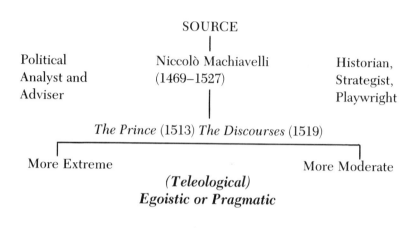

SOURCE

Political Analyst and Adviser

Niccolò Machiavelli (1469–1527)

Historian, Strategist, Playwright

The Prince (1513) *The Discourses* (1519)

More Extreme   More Moderate

(Teleological)
Egoistic or Pragmatic

POWER   **(Cunning-virtù)**   **SUCCESS**

Perspectives on Pragmatic Ethics
Use of normal ethics when workable.
Use of "pragmatics" (what works) if necessary.
Use any means to achieve your end.
Be goal oriented; be persistent/unrelenting.
Be authoritarian, but subtle.
Set the agenda; be self-confident.
Have objectives, vigorously pursued.
Restrict **Fortuna** through **virtù**.*
Don't worry about consequences.
Avoid pity or altruism, unless for self-interest.
Be steadfast, strong, and powerful.

*****Fortuna**—fate—does not only bestow benefits (unlike Providence), but causes setbacks, suffering, etc. Largely beyond human control.
*****Virtù**—human craftiness, virtuosity, cunning: used to offset **Fortuna**.

58

FIGURE 3-2
CONT.

Share power carefully.
Never apologize or admit error, unless it's
expedient.
Always tout Truth—"your truth."
Justice follows power; might is right.
Obey laws if they don't harm your success.
Normal morality: sign of weakness & timidity.
Extol craftiness and cunning; keep ahead of the
lazy masses.
It's better to exploit than to be exploited.
People will believe almost anything.

---

resort to unconventional ethical means. For them, these means
are justified by what they consider a prime journalistic end—
unearthing and providing as much of the truth as possible.

Machiavellianism

This kind of pragmatic journalism might well be referred to
as *Machiavellian* and, indeed, it has been (Merrill, 1992 and
1994). The leading historical exemplar of this kind of pragmatic
ethics is, of course, Niccolò Machiavelli (1469–1527), a Florentine historian and political consultant who believed in success-
oriented (egoistic teleological) ethics (see Figure 3-2). He would
use conventional ethical standards when they worked but would
not refrain from using *any* means if they were needed. Quite
often, Machiavelli did this with grace and charm and with the
demeanor of one who is moderate, reasonable, and well spoken.

It takes no keen observer to see that many journalistic
activities might be called Machiavellian. American journalists,
in seeking their objectives and in achieving their ends, often

59

evidence Machiavellian tendencies. Although we normally associate Machiavelli with evil or destructive ends, such an image may be somewhat unfair. We know that the most socially conscious, altruistic journalists may use Machiavellian tactics from time to time. Such tactics may occasionally be necessary in a hard-nosed, pragmatic, success-oriented journalism.

Let us look for a moment at a modern Machiavellian journalist. Listen to American journalist Robert Sherrill (1986, 17) and consider his words carefully:

> Do journalists sometimes write fiction and pass it off as fact? Do they use stolen material? Tape phone conversations without telling the person on the other end to beware? Misrepresent themselves in order to pry information from reluctant sources? . . . does this mean that journalists are unethical? As one who has done all of the above at one time or another, seldom with a feeling of shame and sometimes with a feeling of satisfaction for the results, I am inclined to pass over the ethical question entirely. If it works, I am generally for it.

This is patently Machiavellian language. How, we might ask, could the journalist justify such thinking? Here is Sherrill's explanation: "So long as reporters, vastly outnumbered and outgunned, are expected to penetrate these hostile areas [government and corporations] to obtain useful information, they can, I think, be forgiven for using almost any device or tactic so long as it enables them to bring back the bacon" (17).

The "bacon," as Sherrill calls it, is the true story. He maintains that journalists often cannot get the true story by normal means because of secrecy and the hostility of sources in government and business. So, for Machiavellians or pragmatic journalists such as Sherrill, professional success overrides conventional ethical practices and often necessitates more extreme means. After all, such journalists maintain, the people need to know.

Here are some examples of Machiavellian practices in journalism: A reporter poses as a mental patient in order to write an exposé of the mental hospital. A reporter surreptitiously records a conversation or interview with a source. An editor gives excessive (and favorable) coverage to a favorite candidate thought best for the community. An editor gives the name of a rape victim in a story, saying that truth or full disclosure is more important than any possible consequences.

Let us not spend too much time on pragmatic ethics. Rather, let us look more closely at humanistic ethics, a less controversial genre of ethical theory. Here we get into the realm of concern for something larger than being successful; here we focus on what is the right or best thing to do, regardless of the consequences to the journalist or press institution. Here we go beyond simply providing the truth to the people. Instead, we begin to consider the consequences of such truth-telling. And we also begin to think about being principled journalists—having foundational tenets or maxims and feeling duty bound to follow them.

Humanistic Ethics

When journalists shift from pragmatics to a more humanistic ethics, they may be motivated by egoism (self-development or self-improvement) or by altruism (concern for others). In either case, of course, there is a strong tendency toward rising above simple expendiency. Humanistic theories of ethics presuppose a desire for social harmony and stability. In other words, humanistic ethics is a form of communitarianism. But, some genres of humanistic ethics also veer in the direction of individualism or libertarianism. As we have pointed out earlier, it is a matter of emphasis. One may have a Platonic proclivity and emphasize the group or the community, or one may have more of an Aristotelian inclination whereby the individual tries to enhance

61

the self for the improvement of the community. Both perspectives would thus fall under the humanistic rubric.

Humanistic ethics can be divided into many subtheories, but here we will discuss three main types: (1) *deontological*, or "duty to principle" ethics; (2) *teleological*, or consequence ethics; and (3) *personalist*, or nonrational, subjective ethics (see Figure 3-3).

Deontological Ethics

Deontological ethics is very appealing because it sets before us definite rules, maxims, or principles that we should follow in order to be ethical. So we have *a priori* guidance (guidance that was conceived beforehand). If we follow the rules, we are ethical; if we break them, we are unethical. Of course, the major problem here is formulating sound, moral rules in the first place. But once we think we have them, our duty is to stick by them. Then we will be principled journalists. A journalist who subscribes to deontological ethics, for example, might believe that a reporter should *always* give the facts without tampering with them, without hiding some of them, and without purposely biasing them in any way.

This journalist would feel unethical if the name of a rape victim were omitted, or if the source of a quote were kept from the story. The "tell the truth" deontologist would be a full-disclosure reporter, feeling an obligation to the public to "tell it the way it is." A journalist with this more professional stance feels a loyalty to the integrity of the story and not to any person connected to the story. This journalist is not concerned with all the possible consequences that might result from the story; these are considered irrelevant to good journalism. Just tell the truth and let the chips fall where they will. After all, the deontologist says, "I am not responsible for results; I am responsible for telling the truth."

Probably the leading deontologist in ethics was Immanuel

FIGURE 3-3
THREE CLASSES OF ETHICAL THEORY

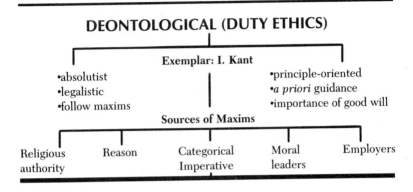

DEONTOLOGICAL (DUTY ETHICS)

Exemplar: I. Kant

•absolutist
•legalistic
•follow maxims

•principle-oriented
•*a priori* guidance
•importance of good will

Sources of Maxims

| Religious authority | Reason | Categorical Imperative | Moral leaders | Employers |

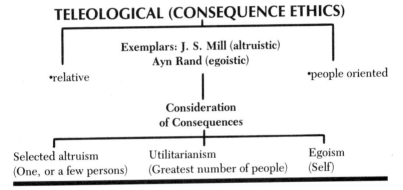

TELEOLOGICAL (CONSEQUENCE ETHICS)

**Exemplars: J. S. Mill (altruistic)
Ayn Rand (egoistic)**

•relative

•people oriented

**Consideration
of Consequences**

| Selected altruism (One, or a few persons) | Utilitarianism (Greatest number of people) | Egoism (Self) |

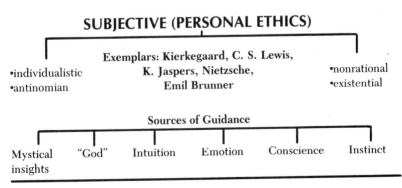

SUBJECTIVE (PERSONAL ETHICS)

**Exemplars: Kierkegaard, C. S. Lewis,
K. Jaspers, Nietzsche,
Emil Brunner**

•individualistic
•antinomian

•nonrational
•existential

Sources of Guidance

| Mystical insights | "God" | Intuition | Emotion | Conscience | Instinct |

63

FOUNDATIONAL MENTOR

Immanuel Kant (1724–1804)

The modern journalist wanting *a priori* guidance for daily journalistic activities will be drawn to Immanuel Kant, one of the modern world's premier philosophers. Kant is perhaps history's best example of a deontological (legalistic, law-oriented, duty-bound) ethicist. He thought that *only* an action taken out of self-imposed duty could be ethical and that consideration of an action's consequences, either to self or to others, wipe out any moral significance such an action might have.

Kant believed in principles, rules, or maxims to which persons (read: journalists) feel it their duty to follow. These would be absolute, rational principles serving as ethical guides. Kantian journalists would not act in order to bring about some kind of consequences. Rather, they would simply act out of a sense of duty to some principle determined ahead of time. Such a principle would be established individually from reason or from rationally developed instinct.

Journalistic rules, freely accepted, would lead to ethical actions. If the journalists follow them, then they are ethical; if not, they are unethical. Such duty-maxims would be categorical—to be followed regardless of the journalists' particular desires at the time. These ethical guidelines would be generated largely by what Kant called his Categorical Imperative, a principle that he believed all rational

Kant (1724–1804), arguably Germany's foremost philosopher (see box, above). It was Kant who has provided the fullest arguments for a "duty to principle" system of morality. The *only* action that can be ethical, he said, is one taken out of self-imposed duty. He formulated what is called the Categorical Imperative,

continued

persons would accept. This imperative is as follows: "Act only according to that maxim by which you can at the same time will that it should become universal law."

Kant also enthroned persons as persons, and his second formulation of the Categorical Imperative demanded that each person be treated as an end and not as a means to some end. The foundations of Kant's ethical system were these: a basic respect for persons and human dignity, and a consistency in following rational maxims with no thought for consequences.

What we probably find most often are journalists who are part Kantian and part consequentialist. On the one hand, they subscribe to *a priori* rules and maxims that they feel duty bound to follow generally. On the other hand, they feel that, on occasion they must make exceptions and take special circumstances into consideration. This, of course, is a rather common ethical position and is legitimized in philosophy under various names, but it does not conform with Kant's thinking. He would consider such a synthesis or *mutualism* as no more than a rationalization for weak-willed and inauthentic journalists. Kant would probably see such an ethical stance as simply a way of trying to please two ethical gods—duty and self-interest. For Kant, in order to have a principled and meaningful ethics, this simply will not work.

which generally stated that what is ethical for a person to do is what that person would have everybody do. This universalizing principle is the genesis of all maxims or rules, largely because, as Kant points out, it is rational. No person would want everyone to go around lying; therefore, lying is unethical.

Another aspect of the famous imperative was that nobody should treat others as means to an end, but only as an end. Certainly this is quite different from Machiavellianism, and it also points up the humanistic nature of Kant's ethics. Together, these two formulations of the Categorical Imperative make up the essence of Kant's "duty to principle" ethics, a theory that is a little too legalistic and cold for many journalists to follow. For many, though, it is a comfortable perspective: It provides guidelines ahead of time to take the agony of decision out of problematic situations as they arise.

Teleological Ethics

The second of the humanistic theories is consequence related, or *teleological*. Teleological ethicists look to the "end" (*telos*), consider the consequences, and speculate about the results of their actions. Teleological journalists do what they feel will best serve society. Or their communities. Or their newspapers. Or themselves. They do what they feel will bring the greatest happiness or benefit to the greatest number (*utilitarianism*). Teleological ethics is primarily seen as an altruistic ethics and is associated with such philosophers as David Hume and James and John Stuart Mill (see box, p. 68) who were known as utilitarians. But another type of teleological ethics can be egoistic, doing what will bring the best consequences to oneself. This latter type of teleology is mainly considered the "dark side" of teleology and is averse to humanism.

However, some ethicists believe that what benefits oneself is quite congenial with what benefits others (Rand, 1964). They believe that when you help yourself, you help others. Rand even says that achieving one's own happiness is a person's highest moral purpose. The seventeenth-century philosopher Thomas Hobbes (1950) defended ethical egoism by connecting it to the Golden Rule: The self is considered first when you think that by doing good things for other, they will do good things to you.

Leonard Peikoff (1983, 308–9), defending Rand's "rational self-interest," stresses that moral selfishness does not mean a license to do what one pleases. What it means, says Peikoff, is a disciplined defining and pursuing of one's *rational* self-interest. It rejects all forms of personal sacrifice, whether this be sacrificing oneself to others or others to oneself. In this sense, the approach could be called humanistic because it upholds reason, independence, honesty, justice, productiveness, self-pride, and integrity.

The journalist who is a teleologist would want to take the action resulting in the most good. To whom? To the party that the actor deems most important. The altruist would think of the good to others; and the egoist would consider some good to oneself, with altruistic benefits flowing out from that. Teleological ethics is very popular because it seems most consistent with a rational concept of morality: One must think before acting, must consider alternatives, and must decide on the best course of action in every case, or in similar cases. The person best known for one version of this theory is the nineteenth-century British philosopher John Stuart Mill. His version of teleology is known as utilitarianism—bringing the greatest happiness to the greatest number. His book *Utilitarianism* is a thorough treatment of this variant of teleology.

Personalist Ethics

Now we come to the third main classification of humanistic ethics, what we are calling personalist theories. The subtheories that embrace ethical personalism are subjective and, for the most part, nonrational. They would involve actions that are intuitive, spiritual, or emotive, based mainly on some kind of feeling or insight of a more transcendental nature. Or, ethical actions stemming from such personal insights would be connected to

John Stuart Mill (1806–1873)

John Stuart Mill is the best known of the nineteenth-century British utilitarians and a successor of the previous century's Englightenment liberal philosophers. A firm defender of personal and political freedom, his essay *On Liberty* (1859) is one of the greatest proclamations on freedom ever written. Mill set the stage for what is now known as libertarianism, a philosophy that has certainly dominated American journalism: "The only freedom which deserves the name, is that of pursuing our own good in our own way, so long as we do not attempt to deprive others of theirs, or impede their efforts to obtain it."

Mill would restrain liberty only for self-protection, or when it might harm others. The problem with this, of course, is that almost anything journalists do may well harm others; it is difficult or impossible for journalists to foresee such harm ahead of time. Today, we are still unsure of the limits of freedom, in spite of Mill's memorable words about it. The debate rages on, as libel suits are brought against journalists, and as philosophers and others debate the nature and scope of freedom.

Other than his rather short essay *On Liberty*, Mill's most influential work was *Utilitarianism* (1861). It pre-

what we normally refer to as conscience. Some small inner voice, unassociated with rational determination, would provide the answers to ethical questions.

Personalist ethics is predicated on a moral sense that pushes us toward right action. For the Christian moralist, this ethical sense may be directed by a concern usually called *agape* love. Kierkegaard's highest level of moral or religious development—the "faith" level—is reached through this kind of love for other

continued

sents his ideas about the "greatest happiness of the greatest number" as a moral principle, which was also called the principle of utility. Mill inherited this concept from Jeremy Bentham and Mill's father, James, who in turn had been influenced by Hobbes and Hume and the French philosopher, Helvetius. John Stuart Mill retained many of the basics of the older utilitarianism, but he humanized it.

In *Utilitarianism,* Mill holds that actions are right in proportion to the degree of happiness they bring. Every person's good is a happiness to that person (an individualist position), and general happiness, Mill said, would flow from individual good to the entire society (a communitarian emphasis). This contention has come in for much criticism, but it remains the foundation for social ethics today.

Mill can teach the modern journalist many things, including (1) that the happiness, good, and welfare of others must be considered; (2) that freedom leads to the general good by providing more avenues for action; (3) that knowledge is always incomplete and a constant effort is needed to get it; and (4) that the freedom to choose and express opinions is necessary if human potential is to be reached.

people. It is also the moving power of Joseph Fletcher's (1966) *situation ethics;* it is this *agape* love (this deep concern for others) that, dominating in any situation, leads to ethical action.

What C. S. Lewis (1952, especially Book III, ch. 3) and others have called conscience and what James Q. Wilson (1993, xii) calls "the moral sense" is another manifestation of personalist ethics. Wilson says that this moral sense is "intuitive or deeply felt . . . about how one ought to act when one is free to act voluntarily." Wilson states that it is not really possible to define such a subjective concept more clearly than that. He mentions the British philosopher Henry Sidgwick (1956), who struggled with the concept of "ought" through half a dozen editions of his great ethics treatise and concluded that the concept "is too elementary to admit of any formal definition" (30).

Another form of personalist ethics is what is sometimes called *antinomianism*—a stance that is against ethical rules or maxims, a kind of reaction against strict Kantian ethics. Several Chinese schools of ethics (such as the Taoist, Zen Buddhist, and Maoist) are compatible with antinomianism because they have little faith in hard and fast ethical commandments. Many persons would consider antinomianism as non-ethics, because it results in an open kind of morality devoid of any *a priori* rules, laws, or guidelines. It is a form of "playing ethics by ear," doing what one's inclinations dictate at the time. This type of ethical system puts freedom above self-restraint and assumes that what comes naturally is the right thing to do.

One form of such an ethics maintains that ethical judgments are only personal preferences and are not really different from various tastes that people have for certain foods. The philosopher A. J. Ayer (1946, 103 and 108), reflecting this position, maintained that because ethical arguments cannot be verified scientifically, they are simply commands or pure expressions of feeling that are devoid of objective validity.

Another type of personalist ethics is existentialism, which we discussed in Chapter 2. Many ethicists contend that there is really no ethical theory of existentialism, or they say that existentialist ethics is so subjective that the term is oxymoronic. Jean-Paul Sartre (1957, 42–43), probably the best-known modern existentialist, emphasizes that we cannot decide ahead of time on an ethics to guide us; he departs from Kant in this respect. Sartre's fellow Frenchman, Albert Camus (see box, p. 72), believed that journalists should seek to change society indirectly through their individual efforts to change themselves. In this belief, Camus differed from Sartre, who was more overtly community minded.

From the writings of Kierkegaard to the present, ethical considerations pervade the works of all existentialists, although the ethics may not be couched in normal moral terminology. Hazel Barnes (1978), a modern American philosopher who is an authority on existentialism, notes that the person who chooses to be unethical rejects the positive assets of freedom. She proclaims that ethics and freedom are both necessary for a worthwhile, fulfilling, and productive life—a life that is of value both to the person and to the society.

For the existential journalist, ethics is personal; it must contribute to the authenticity of the individual. To follow a group-designed code, from either thoughtless habit or blind submission, is depersonalizing and inauthentic. The existentialist must go through the angst of deciding what is right; this decision making creates the essence of each person. What is important is that the existentialist takes personal responsibility for these decisions. And this responsibility imposes a kind of ethical restraint on a person. Another restraint on the existentialist is human dignity; it limits actions for the reason that a person does not live an isolated life. Moral persons have dignity because they constantly try to transcend self and traditional customs.

Friedrich Nietzsche, whom we discussed in Chapter 2, championed the concept of transcendence. He would tell journalists to be positive, to say "yea to life," and to become ever more noble and heroic, rising to their highest potential. Nietzsche strikes a most important existentialist ethical note: Persons are extremely valuable, and they become ever more valuable and worthy as they individually determine their own destinies and repel authority that restricts personal freedom and leads to inauthenticity.

FOUNDATIONAL MENTOR

Albert Camus (1913–1960)

Albert Camus, the French novelist, essayist, and journalist who was born and raised in Algeria, exemplifies the extreme love of freedom and personal development common to the existential tradition. In 1938 he was working as a journalist for several newspapers in both Algeria and France, and during the German occupation of France in World War II, he was active in the French underground press.

Camus, although he didn't call himself one, was a freewheeling existentialist, evidencing in his articles vigor yet restraint, anguish yet hope, historical perspective yet future orientation, individualism yet social awareness. He had a deep respect for facts, coupled with a subjective orientation. He was part mystical artist and part public-conscious social scientist. During the bleak days of World War II, his Parisian newspaper *Combat* was a source of information and encouragement for the anti-Nazi resistance. After the war, Camus continued in journalism by writing for the serious Parisian weekly, *L'Express*, and at the time of his death in an automobile accident in 1960, he was writing for many French newspapers.

What are the main traits of a good journalist? Camus's answer went something like this: a deep concern and re-

A Postscript

In this chapter we have looked at several ethical highways, the main ones being pragmatic and humanistic ethics. Pragmatic ethics, although rational, is problematic, since it is sometimes egocentric or institution-centric. Pragmatic ethics has as its goal the achieving of anticipated ends, and it is basically unconcerned with selfless humanistic actions. Humanistic ethics, on

continued

spect for self, for others, and for the truth; a desire for social progress and personal involvement, coupled with a sense of responsibility, personal commitment, and a deep love of freedom. Camus valued the rebel, but he realized that rebellion—like freedom—implies danger and often isolation. And maturity demands realism and moderation, qualities Camus believed were the prime requirements for good journalism, for every action. Unlike his fellow existentialist Jean-Paul Sartre, Camus would seek to change society indirectly through the individual journalist's efforts to change himself or herself. Sartre would directly change the conditions of people's lives in order to change them individually. Camus was more inner directed, Sartre more other directed. And, although no Communist, Sartre had aligned himself with the Communist party at the very time that other left-wing intellectuals were deserting the party in droves, as Stalin's terrible crimes were documented in the West. As Sartre moved toward the left, Camus became more of an independent, occupying a position similar to that of George Orwell in England. Camus was against all authoritarian regimes and saw Stalin, like Hitler, as personifying evil.

the other hand, has the desire for virtue as its motivation and is largely altruistic in nature.

The pragmatic ethical genre is exemplified in journalism by Machiavellianism, a hard-nosed, success-oriented, competitive journalism that has as its ethical rationale the fulfilling of the people's right to know. However, its freewheeling use of cunning or often secretive means to achieve ends relegates it to a station somewhat lower than normal ethics.

The three main subcategories of humanistic ethics have been designated as deontological (legalistic, duty to principle), teleological (acting out of consideration of consequences), and personalist (subjective, instinctual, religious, existential). The first two are rationalist theories, and the third is nonrational; but they are all driven by virtue. It is quite probable that journalists mix all three of these theories in their everyday work.

Journalists are not simple creatures: They are constantly caught in a dialectic, bouncing at times between pragmatism on one hand and humanism on the other. When they are in the humanistic mode, they may alternately combine Kant's legalism with Mill's utilitarianism; they may also slip from time to time into a personalist ethical state wherein they follow their moral sense or conscience.

Using one's conscience as a guide is generally considered good practice. But, as theologian Paul Tillich (1967, 100–1) points out, there are at least two problems with such a guide. First, he says, there can be a "split conscience," in which two different solutions fight with one another, or in which our courage to take a new step "fights with our bondage to the tradition into which we were indoctrinated." Second, there is what Tillich calls the "erring of conscience." He points out that many of the Nazis in the 1930s and '40s who committed atrocities did so "with good consciences because 'the voice of God,' for them identical with the voice of Hitler, commanded them." Tillich hastens to warn that "no excuse of outer authorities can free us from the burden of decision in the relativities of our human situation." If we do put the burden on an outside authority, secular or religious, Tillich says, we not only "diminish the burden of having to decide, but we also diminish our dignity as persons."

In the next chapter we turn to a most important subject: press freedom and ethics. The seemingly contradictory nature of these two concepts gives rise to many of our basic controversies in journalistic philosophy. We have seen that the communitarians place most of their emphasis on social respon-

sibility, while the libertarians/individualists stress personal responsibility and journalistic freedom. How can free journalists
be responsible? And how free can a journalist be when
haunted by some standard of responsible journalism? This is
the quandary. It is the big question in journalism, not only in
theory but also in practice.

ANALYZING ETHICAL ISSUES

1. Why would journalists be pulled in the direction of pragmatic
   ethics? What is wrong with the kind of Machiavellianism exemplified by journalist Robert Sherrill? What about the ethics of full
   disclosure? Is it a worthy ethical goal or not? Would the Machiavellian journalist always opt for full-disclosure reporting?

2. Do you think there are more journalists who embrace humanistic
   ethics than pragmatic ethics? Of those who are humanists, do you
   think more of them are deontologists or teleologists? Have you
   ever known a journalist who might be called a personalist in ethics? How would you determine what theory (or theories) of ethics
   a journalist is following?

3. Do you consider yourself as primarily a Kantian deontologist or a
   teleologist (either a Millian utilitarian or a Randian rational egoist)? Or, do you feel you have a responsibility to bring good consequences to some other party? Can you make a case for even a
   Kantian actually being a teleologist—at least a kind of *a priori*
   teleologist—who thinks of consequences when formulating guiding maxims or principles?

4. One journalist does one thing (such as giving the name of the rape
   victim). Another journalist does another thing (such as withholding the name of the rape victim). They are both covering the very
   same story. Are both journalists ethical? Are they, in your mind,
   equally ethical?

5. The Golden Rule—"Do unto others as you would have them do unto you"—is often said to be a deontological ethical principle. Do you think it is? How could it be a reliable principle in journalism? If you, a journalist, would not like to have a microphone stuck in your face and asked a long series of questions, then you would refrain from such an action in covering the news. Is that logical? Would you say that the person following the Golden Rule is an altruist or an egoist—thinking mainly of others or mainly of self?

References

Barnes, Hazel. *An Existentialist Ethics.* Chicago: University of Chicago Press, 1978.

Fletcher, Joseph. *Situation Ethics: The New Morality.* Philadelphia: Westminster Press, 1966.

Hobbes, Thomas. *Leviathan.* New York: E. P. Dutton, 1950.

Hudson, Stephen D. *Human Character and Morality.* London: Routledge & Kegan Paul, 1986.

Kant, Immanuel. *Fundamental Principles of the Metaphysics of Morals.* Indianapolis: Bobbs-Merrill, 1949.

Lewis, C. S. *Mere Christianity.* New York: Macmillan, 1952.

Merrill, John C. "Machiavellian Journalism." *Journal of Mass Media Ethics*, vol. 7, no. 2 (1992).

———. "Machiavelli and Press Freedom." *Media Ethics*, vol. 7, no. 1 (fall 1994).

Peikoff, Leonard. *Ominous Parallels.* Briarcliff Manor, NY: Stein & Day, 1983.

Rand, Ayn. *The Virtue of Selfishness.* New York: New American Library, 1964.

Sartre, Jean-Paul. *Existentialism and Human Emotions.* New York: Philosophical Library, 1957.

Sherrill, Robert. "News Ethics: Press and Jerks." *Grand Street* 5 (winter 1986).

Sidgwick, Henry. *The Methods of Ethics*, 7th ed. Indianapolis: Hackett, 1956.

Tillich, Paul. *My Search for Absolutes.* New York: Simon & Schuster (Torchbooks), 1967.

Wilson, James Q. *The Moral Sense.* New York: Free Press, 1993.

CHAPTER FOUR

PRESS FREEDOM AND ETHICS

"Don't tell me what I must do!" snapped the reporter. "Haven't you heard of freedom of the press?"

"So you don't like the way the story was presented?" asks the television news director. "Too bad. You're free to switch channels, but don't interfere with my news judgment."

Every day in the United States journalists hide behind the concept of press freedom to justify their actions. And constitutionally they are within their rights to do so. But as important as freedom is, ethics may well be more important. Walter Lippmann has opined that press freedom is a valid concept only when it leads to the discovery of truth. He has bemoaned the tendency in journalism for "the chaff of silliness, baseness, and deception" to submerge the "kernels of truth."

Freedom clashing with ethics has been a long-standing debate. In opposition to voices like Lippmann's, we can hear Jeremy Bentham, the British utilitarian philosopher, with such questions as these: "Is not liberty to do evil, liberty? If not, what is it? Do we not say that it is necessary to take liberty from idiots and bad men, because they abuse it?" Now, as the century ends, we are left with this problem: How do we protect freedom and at the same time enhance ethics? A daunting problem indeed.

We have seen the various ethical roads journalists may take in their quest of good practice. All these highways and byways, whatever their theoretical foundations, are filtered by the concept of freedom. Why, you may ask, is it necessary to deal with freedom and ethics at the same time? The answer is easy. The two concepts are closely related in a somewhat contradictory way; down through the years, philosophers have recognized this and have tried to reconcile them. It is often difficult. Although freedom can work against ethical conformity, it is also true in philosophy that freedom is an assumption for any kind of ethical action.

One must be substantially free in order for ethical choice to be possible. One must have the freedom to choose between or among alternative actions: This is the *sine qua non* of ethics. As Herbert Muller (1960, 49) has written, free people must "do something with their freedom, employing it to some purpose." He also observes that as "they become freer, have more choice in ends, their most difficult problems begin."

Freedom: Both Essential and Dangerous

For the journalist, the whole idea of press freedom opens the door to responsible and irresponsible actions—in short, to media ethics. At the same time, press freedom forces upon ethical consideration a certain relativity—and even a substantial contradiction—that often proves to be a nemesis to ethical resolution.

It is important to recognize that freedom of expression is essential, albeit somewhat dangerous, to any meaningful concept of communication ethics. Herbert Altschull (1990, 27) writes that "an ethical choice cannot be other than a free one; otherwise, one cannot be held responsible for one's actions." Why, then, is freedom sometimes viewed as an obstacle? Here is one reason: Robert Bellah and his coauthors (1985, 76) express the belief that freedom (or at least, individual autonomy) makes it difficult, if not impossible, to conceive of any "objectifiable criteria of right and wrong, good or evil" that all of us can hold in common. Press freedom is, indeed, painful to many people. In the abstract, the concept may be appealing, but when the press wades into our "sacred" areas of concern and tramples on our deeply held values, we have some doubts about the benefits of freedom. We are dedicated to our own freedom but often have doubts about the freedom of others. Nat Hentoff (1993, 386) a modern journalist who loves freedom of expression, has serious doubts about the people's support for such freedom. He sums up the question well: "As for ratification, imagine the First Amendment of the ballot. It is very doubtful whether it could be reaffirmed in many places without such qualifications as 'freedom of speech, or of the press—except for racist, anti-Catholic, sexist, anti-Semitic, homophobic and any other language offensive to any ethnic or religious groups.' "

Limits to Freedom of Expression?

In late 1993, when U.S. attorney general Janet Reno warned the media to desist in their violent programming or expect government action, many media exploded with editorial cries of alarm. It was obvious, however, that their audiences did not share their passion for the First Amendment. There is a growing belief that much of what is expressed these days as "free speech" should not be protected by the Constitution and that uninhibited speech does present some kind of "clear and present danger" to the moral fiber of the country. A growing public sense is emerging that something has to be done about what is seen as the viciousness and distortion that flood into our homes and corrupt our children's ideals. Few doubt that the media share, more than ever before, a great responsibility for the deepest notions our children have of what is proper, or at least acceptable, social conduct.

79

Cass Sunstein (1993) notes that actually we have three
kinds of speech (or media messages): (1) that which is censored,
politically banned or punished, or unfree for political reasons;
(2) free speech, on which democracy depends, the kind the
U.S. Constitution protects because it permits citizens to criti-
cize government and bureaucrats; and (3) "sold speech," or
"second-tier" speech—that pertaining to subjects not related to
governance and not worth defending at the expense of social
morality.

Even the noted German educational philosopher Wilhelm
von Humboldt (1767–1835), a lover of freedom and champion of
individuality, indicated an ambivalence about society and individuality, restraint and freedom. Although a firm believer in
individualism, von Humboldt saw the advantages of social controls. His concept of *Bildung* (harmonious individuality nourished by diverse experiences) evidenced a dialecticism inherited
from his study of his fellow countryman, the philosopher Hegel.
Von Humboldt was seeking a meaningful synthesis or middle
ground, not so coldly rational as Kant, but not so romantically
emotional as Rousseau; not so freedom oriented as Milton or
Voltaire, but not so authoritarian as Machiavelli or Hobbes.

However, von Humboldt (1993, 12–13) seemed to be
caught up in the individualism-freedom emphasis of the dialectic, as demonstrated in the following passage:

> Individual vigour . . . and manifold diversity combine
> themselves in originality; and hence, that on which the
> whole greatness of mankind ultimately depends—to-
> wards which every human being must ceaselessly direct
> his efforts, and of which especially those who wish to
> influence their fellow-men must never lose sight: indi-
> viduality of energy and self-development. . . . The high-
> est ideal . . . of the co-existence of human beings seems
> to me to consist in a union in which each strives to
> develop himself from his own inmost nature, and for his
> own sake.

Although von Humboldt had no misconceptions about the importance of order, discipline, law, and the networks that make up a community, he almost always came down on the side of individualism. Here is another statement that seems to emphasize his basic tendency: "Now, whatever man receives externally is only like the seed. It is his own active energy alone that can turn the most promising seed into a full and precious blessing for himself. It is beneficial only to the extent that it is full of vital power and essentially individual" (13).

Freedom for "Silliness and Baseness"?

Can one imagine Madison or Jefferson trying to protect much of the "sold speech" (referred to earlier by Sunstein) that engulfs us? And can one imagine Jefferson favoring any "seeds" other than von Humboldt's "promising" ones that produce vital power and a blessing for the individual? Wayne Booth (1993, 10-a), professor emeritus of English at the University of Chicago, points out that these Founding Fathers wanted to protect democratic discourse, the "absolute right of speakers to express their own genuine convictions." This, Booth adds, is quite different from the right to express "what one knows to be false or harmful."

Walter Lippmann (1955, 97–100) deals with this problem of freedom of expression in a similar vein. What he stresses as the rationale for such freedom is the discovery of truth. "It is only from the hope and the intention of discovering truth," he writes, "that freedom acquires such high public significance." Then he adds:

> But when the chaff of silliness, baseness, and deception is so voluminous that it submerges the kernels of truth, freedom of speech may produce such frivolity, or such mischief, that it cannot be preserved against the demand for a restoration of order or of decency. If there is a divid-

81

ing line between liberty and license, it is where freedom
of speech is no longer respected as a procedure of the
truth and becomes the unrestricted right to exploit the
ignorance, and to incite the passions, of the people.

Despite the patent good sense of such remarks as Lippmann's, most journalists today think of freedom as a sacred and
even unrestricted right, and they think much more about freedom than about responsible choices. As we noted earlier, however, this is changing. Journalistic concern is being thrust into a
new direction—away from the rights of the press and toward the
responsibilities of the press. Accompanying this shift from freedom to ethics is a new emphasis on social imperatives rather than
individual imperatives. The older emphasis, stemming from European thought of the seventeenth and eighteenth centuries,
always placed the emphasis on the individual and on liberty. The
"thinking self," launched dramatically by René Descartes with
his well-known principle "I think, therefore I am," has largely
dominated Western philosophy and journalism.

The pure or extreme position of Enlightenment thought
about freedom was expressed by the Frenchman Benjamin Constant. Constant emphasized the importance of the self and the
self-determination of expression, demanding a maximum degree of nonintervention in press freedom. Constant saw clearly
that shifting authority from one group to another does nothing
to increase liberty; it simply changes the burden of slavery.
Whether the journalist, for example, is restricted by a mon-
arch, a popular government, oppressive laws, or even by a
tyrannical publisher makes little difference so far as freedom is
concerned. In this regard, Constant was also suspicious of democracy. He said that democracy "may disarm a given oligar-
chy, a given privileged individual, or set of individuals, but it
can still crush individuals as mercilessly as any previous ruler"
(Berlin, 163–64).

The "self" of the Enlightenment began to lose some of its

luster in the nineteenth century, and progressively during the twentieth century it was fading away in the face of increased emphasis on socialization, collectivization, cooperation, institutionalization, social engineering, and the development of a sense of community. Especially in Asia, where the society and harmonious social interaction and cooperation have been prized for centuries, the highest value is placed not on the individual but on the social unit. In their value systems, Asians find social adaptation and group solidarity far more attractive than the individualism still revered by many in the West.

An Asian Perspective

The Asian countries now caught in the throes of rapid economic development (South Korea, Taiwan, Japan, and Singapore, for example) have all been influenced profoundly by Confucian thought (see box, p. 84), which treats individuals as inferior to society. According to Confucianism (see Confucius's *Analects*), a person is born into a particular society and develops and reaches maturity within it, being in a sense created by it. "Be filial to your parents and loyal to your master," says Confucius (Wilson, 1993, 197). Such a philosophy naturally leads to a more adaptive and less individualistic stance. The weight of value is on the side of society, and a person's existence has meaning only to the degree that it fulfills the role society assigns. In Confucianism, then, we see an early form of communitarianism.

Even more than Confucius, the fifth-century Chinese thinker Mo Tzu stressed a sense of community and even universal love. He believed, like Plato, in having only worthy men in government and respecting one's superiors as a means of having uniform moral standards (Tseu, 1962, 50–95). Mo Tzu believed in the collective solution of social problems and was opposed to Confucian fatalism. He advocated an intellectual aristocracy, believing that people were not born equal and that

Confucius (551–479 B.C.)

Confucius's main advice to journalists would be that they must reach full moral and professional maturity by being effective and cooperative members of their group, their medium, their profession. Confucian philosophy would have journalists inclined toward an adaptive and socially involved kind of journalism, what today might be termed a kind of communitarianism. In many ways (see his *Analects*), Confucius was similar to Plato in saying that a person should sublimate self to the collective and have a kind of group loyalty.

As with modern communitarians, the weight of value, in Confucianism, is on the side of society, and the journalists' work would have meaning so far as it fulfills the role assigned within the medium or profession. The emphasis is on individual adaptation to the group. As for freedom, the Confucian view is that one has the freedom to choose good—not evil. Thus, modern journalists would have the freedom to be responsible, not irresponsible.

Confucianism for journalists is an alternative to the Western—especially Protestant—values of rugged individualism, sacrifice, and self-promotion. Many modern

only the wise and able few should rule; creeds and directions from above should be respected without question from below, so that there could be social solidarity. It is not surprising that Mao Zadong and his successors in the Chinese Communist party have held the concepts of Mo Tzu in high regard.

One can easily see where this social-adaptation philosophy leads: to a more socially defined ethics, to a conformist press system, and to an increased desire for a greater certainty (or absolutism) in media ethics. The society or the community is

continued

journalists—especially in the West—steeped in the ideas of personal autonomy and libertarianism, would see great dangers in Confucian journalism. But it is simply an alternative way of looking at society and social institutions, wherein stability, dignity, and the value of the social unit take precedence over the individual.

Confucian journalists would act habitually, out of respect for others and a desire for social stability. Virtues would be learned and developed and come into play naturally when needed for moral action. Especially important in Confucian ethics are the virtues of work, courtesy, empathy, and consideration. Confucian news reporters would think of others connected with a story: There would be no invasion of privacy; nothing that would bring shame or grief; no using of people as a means to an end; and no emphasis on superficial, negative, or sensational stories.

Confucius would see the journalist as maximizing social harmony, accentuating the positive, and expanding the total discourse of civility and rationality. For Confucius, the journalist would be first of all a *person in community* and secondly a journalist.

enthroned, and the individual is relegated to a minor role, one of being a cooperating and harmonious cog in the social machine.

What has just been said is simply a description of what many libertarians see as the ethical shift that is under way. Freedom, according to the communitarians, is considered dangerous, whereas social cohesion and harmony are considered beneficial and desirable. Freedom, of course, implies the individual determination of ethical standards and actions, and this can be—and often is—disruptive or traumatic to a society, a nation, a newspaper, or even a family. Many important Eastern as well as Western philosophers have noted this problem and have pointed to a need for a more coherent morality, one that stresses personal cooperation with the group and adherence to its collective norms.

A Look at Press Freedom

Although in the West the social or communitarian shift has not proceeded as far as in some Asian countries, it has made significant inroads, especially in Germany and Scandinavia. And it is probable that the former communist nations of Eastern Europe and the political entities of the Commonwealth of Independent States (Russia and some parts of the former Soviet Union) will not forsake the spirit of community and social cooperation that marked their existence for half a century.

In the West, the individualistic spirit and press libertarianism that spread throughout the Enlightenment and well into the late nineteenth century has, in modern times, been faced with a growing skepticism and opposition. As the theory of social responsibility took root in the mid-twentieth century (recall the Hutchins Commission recommendations discussed in Chapter 1), the stress was taken off press freedom. After all, how can we really concentrate on press *ethics* if we keep our earlier focus on press *freedom?*

European Enlightenment philosophers of the seventeenth and eighteenth centuries thought they lived in the best of times and worlds; nature seemed good and people rational. There was optimism, and progress seemed inevitable. Reason was definitely on the throne, and occultism, religion, and emotionalism remained in the shadows. Although the spirit of the Age of Reason did not last very long in the overall sweep of history, it did have a powerful impact. If nothing else, it reached into the early American colonies and into the newly created American nation. It influenced Franklin, Jefferson, Madison, Hamilton, Jay, and others (people who valued rationalism and individualism and, most important of all for the press, freedom of expression). Remnants of Enlightenment libertarianism survived into the early nineteenth century, and still exist in scattered places and in a weaker form. Let us look again at John Stuart Mill, a significant figure who supported the Enlightenment stance.

Mill's Classic Case for Freedom and Stephen's Reply

As we noted in earlier chapters, John Stuart Mill is counted among the greatest champions of freedom, especially freedom of expression. But Mill was not an absolutist; if freedom causes social harm, Mill thought it should be circumscribed. Whereas John Locke believed freedom of the press was a God-given natural right, Mill saw freedom in utilitarian terms: What could it do to bring about happiness or good in a society? He also believed that his freedom principle was appropriate only in societies of relatively high educational standards, in which people could *rationally* exercise such freedom.

Mill's classic essay *On Liberty* best sets forth his views on freedom of expression. He wrote: "If all mankind minus one were of one opinion, and only one person were of the contrary opinion, mankind would be no more justified in silencing that one person, than he, if he had the power, would be justified in silencing mankind" (1974, 16). According to Albert W. Levi (1966, 12), Mill believed that only through free expression could a person attain rational and moral perfection. And, says Levi, Mill's stress on self-realization and the pluralism of messages shows clearly that "the spirit of his concepts might well be a digest of the related parts of the *Nicomachean Ethics* of Aristotle."

Fourteen years after Mill's *On Liberty* was published, James Fitzjames Stephen's *Liberty, Equality, Fraternity* (1882) appeared. Stephen's book, which has proved to be the best critique directed at Mill, injected the communitarian stance that an individual cannot exercise freedom in a vacuum. A person, wrote Stephen, must consider freedom as it relates to others. He accused Mill of putting too much stress on an individualistic ethic, which was somewhat strange in light of Mill's utilitarianism, and believed that Mill should have given more attention to personal interaction.

Compared to Mill, Stephen takes a far more moderate view of freedom. His concept of freedom avoids absolutes and veers toward a position that takes responsibility into consideration. Stephen wrote that we "must proceed in a far more cautious way, and confine ourselves to such remarks as experience suggests about the advantages and disadvantages of compulsion and liberty respectively in particular cases" (Radcliff, 1966, 50).

Stephen (1993, 30), in his attack on Mill's concept of liberty, made three main points countering Mill's contentions in *On Liberty:*

1. The growth of liberty, like democracy, tends to diminish, not increase, originality and individuality; it is like plucking a bird's feathers to make it equal with beasts, and then ordering it to fly.
2. The hope that people will become more vigorous by simply removing restrictions is as fallacious as the hope that a bush planted in an open field will naturally develop into a forest tree.
3. Although goodness may be pluralistic, variety is not in itself good (e.g., a nation in which all citizens were sober would be happier, better, and more progressive, though less diverse, than one in which half the citizens were sober and the other half were drunkards).

Opposing Mill's enthroning of freedom, Stephen (1993, 34–35) writes that the "question whether liberty is a good or a bad thing appears as irrational as the question whether fire is a good or a bad thing." Freedom is, according to Stephen, both good and bad "according to time, place, and circumstance," and is not a "very simple principle" with absolute goodness as Mill suggests.

Enlightenment Perspectives on Freedom

In the late eighteenth century and well into the nineteenth century, a majority of serious thinkers in Europe gave full appreciation to the concept of freedom. This concern with freedom did not remain on an intellectual level but spilled over into economics, politics, and the general social domain. Advocates of freedom made this main argument: A free press functions to present the truth, however splintered it may be, in a diversity of voices. It is impossible to do this if the press is controlled by some authority, or if restrictions of some type dissipate editorial self-determination. This is the basic libertarian approach, one that sees the best press as one working in a laissez-faire, unfettered situation, which leads to an abundance of information and a pluralism of viewpoints necessary in a democratic society.

John Milton and John Locke

Long before John Stuart Mill, the British were staunch supporters of freedom. Let us look briefly at two of them as a key to Enlightenment thought. Perhaps the earliest of the great documents pointing out the value of freedom of expression was John Milton's *Areopagitica* (1664). In it he proposed his well-known self-righting principle, which has stood for centuries as a justification for a free press as it is understood under capitalism. Milton assumed that people are rational and wise enough to know right from wrong, good from bad. This being the case, people should be free from government control of their expression. Unless they have free choice in communication, believed

89

John Locke (1632–1704)

Responsible individualism, predicated on a love of reason and the importance of natural law, was stressed by the late-seventeenth-century English philosopher John Locke. One of Europe's premier thinkers, Locke lived at a time when England was attempting great political reform, seeking to limit the power of the royalty, establish a parliament, and secure religious freedom. John Locke was a major player in these efforts—both politically and philosophically.

Lockean journalists would be more than information gatherers; they would be concerned, intelligent, and rational. Locke strikes an existential note in his belief that a person is made or constituted by actions and the awareness of the self-actualized self. Ethical journalists, according to Locke, are those who act only after serious thought about what is right and good. Locke saw moral laws as ultimately founded in God's law.

A person cannot be ethical *by chance*, Locke would say. In this view, he seems to contradict Aristotle and Confucius, because he believed that a person could not be ethical simply out of habit. According to Locke, moral consequences may result from habitual action, but to act ethically one must act *self-consciously*. The journalist, for instance, who habitually (without thinking about the par-

Milton, people could not fully exercise their reason. Milton also believed that, given a free and open encounter, truth will defeat error. This is the core of Milton's self-righting principle, which is still a force in the mass consciousness of the West, although it is increasingly being challenged by antiliberals.

Another important British philosopher was John Locke

continued

ticular case) omits the name of a rape victim from a story is simply acting automatically, not ethically.

What are the sources of Locke's ethical guidelines? There are two sources, indicating two aspects of his character and value system: (1) biblical guidelines and (2) discovery—through reason—of moral laws. Basically, Locke considered being moral as being rational.

Locke was an early libertarian, seeing freedom as essential to full human development. Freedom, for Locke, was a natural right—good *per se,* not so that it might contribute to some social benefit, as John Stuart Mill would later assert. Freedom for Locke is, of course, never complete since individuals live in society and need order, not anarchy, for their own benefit. Reason serves as an automatic control of freedom. So that individuals can live orderly and moral lives—the essence of humanity—rational people place limits on their freedom. Such rational control of freedom, for Locke, is what differentiates humans from the "savage beasts" that exist on a lower level. Freedom must be tempered by reason, and journalists, for instance, would have no right to freedom unless it were guided by reason. Locke, then, was certainly not a pure libertarian; very important strings were attached to his idea of freedom.

(1632–1704), who is generally considered the leading philosopher of the Enlightenment (see box, p. 90). His ideas set the tone for many of the philosophers who followed, and it was Locke's love of freedom that so greatly influenced the Founding Fathers of the American republic. Liberty was very important to Locke. He saw it as a *natural* right, one that should not be abridged except when it might interfere with the liberty of another. He also saw government as being a creation of, and servant of, the people. There is little doubt about the considerable influence of Locke on such thinkers as Jefferson and Paine in early America and on the *philosophes* Voltaire and Montesquieu in France.

Locke stressed the sanctity of the individual, the rule of law, checks and balances in government, and the rule of reason in human affairs. He believed that the mind is capable of finding the truth. He saw the need for maximum freedom for the individual if the mind were to do its proper work.

A Shift Sets In

While Locke was enthroning reason, other important figures were planting seeds of subjectivism (idealism and mysticism) in the philosophical fields. Romanticism was beginning to make itself felt in the dominant rationalist intellectual environment. But even in the seventeenth century, Thomas Hobbes, while paying lip service, like Locke, to freedom of expression, was opening the door to a deemphasis of individualism. Hobbes, who has been called the father of modern democratic theory, believed that human nature required outside direction. This is why he proposed a sovereign (his *Leviathan*) with absolute power to curb people's use of freedom and to keep them from being irresponsible and harming society. Here was one of the earliest intellectual proponents of one form of the incipient communitarian movement. Hobbes was still generally in the liberal mode of his day, but the stage was being set for a shift away from the individual and personal freedom.

There was also Jean-Jacques Rousseau (1712–1778) in France, who talked about liberty (coining the slogan "liberty, fraternity, and equality") while at the same time fostering the terrorism of the French Revolution. Despite Rousseau's basic affinity for freedom, he came to the position that each person, for everyone's sake, must give up freedom and power to the state and obey the collective will.

His fellow countryman Benjamin Constant considered Rousseau the most dangerous enemy of individual freedom, because Rousseau had declared that each person should give up self to the collective, but justified it by saying that "by giving myself to all I give myself to none" (Berlin, 1969, 164). Rousseau, according to Constant, would turn the clock back to Plato, with the collective will taking the place of the philosopher king. But he would also foreshadow the present, when communitarians are preaching the importance of the collective will and a social gospel of social adaptation.

During the nineteenth century, the emphasis on freedom, rationality, and individuality was still getting considerable but sporadic support (from philosophers such as Mill and Tocqueville). Hegel, in Germany, was discussing freedom while predicting its demise; he saw individual freedom going through stages, always diminishing through history, and coming finally to a third stage (old age) wherein social aims absorb all individual aims. The Frenchman Alexis de Tocqueville (see box, p. 94) adhered to the older libertarian school, as shown in his important work, *Democracy in America* (1835). Tocqueville believed that freedom produces a recognition of the importance of the individual and that it provides people with great energy and a love for pursuing their own interests and passions. Peter Lawler (1991, 25) says of Tocqueville that he considered liberty as "a mixture of the truth and error, of reason, passion, or instinct, that constitutes human life," and that it affirmed the tensions and contradictions of body and soul—a mixture that he called "the beast with an angel in him."

Most philosophers of the nineteenth and twentieth centuries have paid respect to the mode of individual freedom, but they increasingly have stressed that they do not believe in

Alexis de Tocqueville (1805–1859)

Journalists who want an outside view of American democracy and the press should read Tocqueville's *Democracy in America,* which was published in France in 1835 and 1840. Alexis de Tocqueville came to America in 1831, ostensibly to study the penal system. He traveled from New York to the limits of the country's western expansion, and from Canada to New Orleans. He was mainly interested in American democracy and how it worked.

The book was an immediate success and propelled Tocqueville to fame in Europe. It contains keen insights into American society and hints at problems that would later arise from the American experience with democracy. It is arguably the finest depiction of the spirit of America, and it is a major work in political theory.

Tocqueville deals with press freedom in the United States. He gives a good contrast of French and American newspapers, one that is probably as true today as it was in the 1800s. In France, newspapers gave very limited space to advertising, whereas some three-quarters of the papers in America were filled with advertisements. In France, the papers devoted considerable space to "passionate discussions," whereas American papers gave mainly "political intelligence and trivial anecdotes."

absolute freedom and have been proposing various restrictions on it. It is true that some, like today's anarchists or radical libertarians, come close to advocating absolute freedom, but they always impose some limits. Most present-day intellectuals who deal with the subject of freedom and ethics take a position close to that of the social critic and neoconservative, Robert Nisbet (1953), who has declared that although freedom is im-

continued

American newspapers, in Tocqueville's view, abused the powers of thought and serious intellectual concern. He disliked newspapers' coarse appeals to the passions, assaults on the character of individuals, and invasion of privacy, and he observed that newspapers pointed out all sorts of negative things about people. He said that persons of esteem and authority in America are afraid to write in the newspapers (unlike in France), and they are thereby deprived of the "most powerful instrument which they can use to excite the passions of the multitude to their own advantage."

Personal opinions of American editors carry no weight with the American public, Tocqueville opined. What the public wants in a newspaper is factual knowledge, and the only way journalists can support their own views is by changing or distorting facts. Modern American journalists may certainly take exception to that observation, pointing out that this situation has changed significantly, with editorials, columns, letters, and op-ed pieces now having a high readership. Perhaps modern journalists can learn little of importance about ethics *per se* from Tocqueville, but they can appreciate his precise and astute reporting and analysis, and they can enjoy the directness and clarity of his language.

portant, it is but one of several values necessary in a good and just society. According to Nisbet, freedom not only may but must "be restricted when such freedom shows signs of weakening or endangering national security, of doing violence to the moral order and the social fabric" (Carey, 1984, 4). This position sounds very much like that of the communitarians, discussed in Chapter 1.

Libertarianism: Remnants

In spite of this shift away from an emphasis on freedom, the libertarians are still with us today. Their basic position is that of the Enlightenment writers and might be expressed in the words of philosopher John Hospers (Carey, 1984, 65): "Leave the individual alone." (The press libertarian's motto would then be "Leave the press alone.") As expressed by Harvard philosopher Robert Nozick (1974), libertarians believe in the minimal ("night-watchman") state where, under limited government, most of an individual's decisions—unless they violate the rights of others—can be freely made. Today's libertarians, exemplified by such writers as Hospers and Nozick, Tibor Machan, Jerome Tuccille, and Murray Rothbard, would caution journalists to approach any kind of groupism very cautiously and to be always ready to fight against what they see as an invidious extension of institutional power into the lives of individuals.

The radical and extremely popular American personal journalist I. F. Stone (1907–1989) was a prominent champion of freedom of expression. Kant's Categorical Imperative ("Act only according to that maxim by which you can at the same time will that it should become universal law") was at the core of Stone's ethical approach. Behind his ethics stood freedom, and he was dedicated to it. Journalism educator Jack Lule (1993, 95), writing about Stone's ethics, emphasizes Stone's belief that journalists had "not only the right but the responsibility to defend freedom of expression."

Believing that journalists should freely choose their own ethical standards and guidelines and stick to them, Stone rejected expediency, dismissed situational concerns, and frowned on "a too careful calculation of consequences" (Lule, 98). Even the people he attacked recognized that Stone's standards were clear and precise and were offered with few reservations. He was a strict constructionist ("freedom of expression is freedom of expression—period") when it came to the First Amendment freedom of the press.

Some modern observers do not take such a "radical" view of press freedom. H. Eugene Goodwin (1983, 5), a professor at Pennsylvania State University, has written that "it must be understood that the First Amendment does not literally mean that no laws whatever can be passed abridging freedom of the press." He notes that libel and slander laws have been permitted. But Goodwin observes that there are free press "absolutists" and he gives several examples: Abe Rosenthal, former editor of the *New York Times*, Jack Landau, director of the Reporters' Committee for Freedom of the Press, and Lyle Denniston, Supreme Court reporter for the *Baltimore Sun.*

Goodwin goes on to say that Denniston, for example, was unable to accept a universal ethical code for journalists, and that he saw the First Amendment as providing "a social value preference for an open society in which there cannot be any governmental restraints on the communication of ideas" (6). Beyond that, Goodwin says, Denniston holds that even industry ethics codes are alien to his basic notion about free expression of ideas, and that journalistic ethics have to be individual—"based on some kind of internal moral-ethical perception" (6).

The American libertarian in the twentieth century, in addition to receiving support from the Constitution, has drawn intellectual sustenance from existentialism. As we noted in earlier chapters, for the existentialist, the self and its enhancement top the list of priorities. Existentialists such as Kierkegaard, Nietzsche, Jaspers, Marcel, Camus, Sartre, Heidegger, Berdyaev, and Ortega y Gasset have all expressed concern about the disappearance of the authentic self, about the tendency of mass society to swallow up the person in a kind of dehumanizing system. They warn that by sacrificing self to a collective, one becomes an inauthentic person. To escape this kind of existence, a person must fight constantly to create a self and to oppose any attempt to limit personal freedom, so that the person will not become, as

97

Journalism Ethics

Ortega y Gasset put it, "like a stone which is given its own existence" (Kaufmann, 1975, 153–54).

In spite of the legacy of the Enlightenment, the forcefulness of a series of voices defending freedom, the refusal of libertarianism to die, and the spirited influence of existentialism, the shift from freedom to responsibility appears to be continuing. At least in some prominent academic circles, the opinion seems to be that the old liberal emphasis on freedom and individualism is detrimental to the development of journalistic ethics. In the media themselves the change is coming more slowly. We will look at this new social consciousness, which is attempting to change the very foundations of American journalism.

Escape from Freedom to Ethics

Today some American intellectuals, in the media and in the universities, believe that the media need to escape from their exaggerated concern for freedom inherited from the European Enlightenment. Advocates of a meaningful ethics maintain that the time has come for the media to develop a sense of responsibility—a more absolute concept of ethics—that precludes the fractionalizing and relativizing of journalistic actions. Many ethics specialists (especially the communitarians) today are advising media and journalists to "escape from freedom" (Fromm, 1965) into a socially responsible network of cooperation and harmony.

Freedom, of course, must be retained, or at least an indeterminate amount of it must be kept. For, as was pointed out in Chapter 1, a certain degree of freedom is necessary even for a discussion of ethics. But the freedom that is stressed today in journalistic circles concerned with media ethics is what is generally called *positive freedom* (or active freedom), which is freedom for the media to react responsibly to social concerns and needs. The older concept of *negative freedom* (passive freedom, or freedom from outside control or direction), now associated by some with a discredited libertarianism initiated by the Enlightenment, is today often looked upon as sterile and socially unproductive or even harmful.

In summary, we find that the philosophical emphasis is first on ethics or media responsibility to society, second on positive freedom (the freedom to act positively), and last on negative freedom (freedom from extra-media coercion). As we push ever further into the area of ethics, we are faced with the problem of finding standards or principles to guide us in our journalism. The questions arise: What are these standards? Where do we get them? Some of the answers to such questions were given in Chapter 3 as we surveyed various ethical theories. And, as we said in that chapter, the sensible ethicist will use all or useful parts of the theories.

Guided Freedom: Eclecticism

Perhaps journalists should accept some kind of eclectic moral philosophy in journalism, such as the one proposed by Professor Edmund Lambeth (1992, 23), which he says should include Judeo-Christian values and those of the classical Greeks. Lambeth notes that such an eclectic system of ethics would "reflect working principles rather than platitudes" or simple "dos and don'ts." Lambeth would want some flexibility in such a system, but not too much, for he believes that an ethical system shouldn't be so flexible as to "be a mere rationalization for the personal preferences of those who invoke it. In short, a system must have bite and give direction. Its precepts should offer continuity and stability" (24).

Although Lambeth, like the communitarians, is retreating from libertarianism, he would still admit considerable freedom in his ethical system. This system, as he says, is closest to what he calls "mixed rule deontology" (24), in which journalists con-

sider consequences while at the same time they are guided by
rules derived from principles—a kind of synthesis of John Stuart Mill and Immanuel Kant. This is virtually the same system
that Merrill (1989) calls "deontelic ethics." The important thing
here, and what saves Lambeth's system from being completely
ignored by libertarians, is that personal freedom does indeed
enter in. A person can, using freedom, try to think through the
various alternative actions, anticipate consequences, and tailor
individual ethical decisions. At the same time, libertarians
might wonder what Lambeth means by an ethical system "having bite" and offering "continuity and stability." These statements, like many of the broad generalizations of the Hutchins
Commission, have certain authoritarian implications, or at least
cause some interesting semantic problems.

Freedom: Persistent Ethical Problem

Every time some ethicist proposes a more absolute social
ethics, one that might well offer "continuity and stability," the
ghosts of the Enlightenment thinkers loom up to confound any
effort to frame a monolithic normative moral guide that would
be meaningful and binding on the media. Voices of Locke,
Kant, Voltaire, Hume, and Adam Smith are heard warning of
encroaching authoritarianism. As James Q. Wilson says (1993,
196–97), although the ethics of communalism, tradition, and
self-control have largely remained the dominant ethos in all
other parts of the world, the Enlightenment commitment to
"skeptical reason, personal freedom, and self-expression" has
persisted in Western Europe and America.

This legacy of rationalism, individualism, and freedom has
been a persistent barrier to media ethics. The media person is
pulled constantly in two directions: toward following a group-
determined or at least majoritarian ethics, and toward following
self-imposed and often minoritarian ethics. On the one hand,
there seems to be a strong proclivity in American journalists for

what has been common in many parts of the world—a reliance on custom, on communal harmony and conformity, on rigorous and existing legal codes of conduct, and on a doctrine of collective responsibility. But alongside that tendency is the persistent Enlightenment strain of individualism and freedom, which enthrones independence, self-enhancement, and the acceptance of personal responsibility.

Wilson (1993, 197) wonders why the Enlightenment occurred in the West and nowhere else, and why in the West, to a much greater degree than anywhere else, there has been such a commitment to individualism, freedom, and respect for personal autonomy. He further questions why "we in the West" believe that when arbitrary power is overthrown and each individual seeks his or her own ethics, the result inevitably will be socially good. This is the same sort of question being asked increasingly by communitarians and other social ethicists, who see individualism and libertarianism as leading to a chaotic and often socially destructive ethics.

Libertarianism is, indeed, under attack. One reason, as Paul Lutz so clearly points out, is that libertarianism "is incomplete as a moral philosophy and remains seriously in need of repair unless it is willing to modify its ethical system so that it can introduce deontological considerations" (Carey, 1984, 143). Edward B. McLean also takes a shot at libertarianism: "Liberty per se is not valuable, for it has no moral value unless it is considered in terms of how it is to be used and for what it is to be used" (48).

Many great thinkers through the ages have noted the dangerous aspects of freedom and have pointed out the socially injurious nature of democracy. History is full of warnings about the dangers of social atomism and the arrogance of individualism; it also offers examples of the social value of harmonious cooperation and the deemphasis of personal autonomy for the smooth running of the communal system.

Despite such warnings, however, and the fact that we see in

our media system a chaotic hodgepodge of often conflicting ethical beliefs and actions, the individualism of the Enlightenment is still potent. It stands as a pluralistic barrier against the development of a consensual, monolithic, absolute, normative ethics for the American mass media. How long this individualist emphasis on freedom will continue to thwart a meaningful social or communitarian ethics is anyone's guess.

ANALYZING ETHICAL ISSUES

1. Some people contend that journalistic freedom opens the door to unethical actions, that freedom and ethics are not compatible. Do you agree with this contention? Why or why not? Discuss how a journalistic ethics could exist in a society in which no press freedom was permitted. Do you feel that the former Soviet Union or Hitler's Germany produced a highly ethical press? Could a non-free journalistic system still be ethical? Explain how this might be possible.

2. If a journalist has no freedom to choose among alternative actions, can he or she be ethical—or unethical? Why or why not might an authoritarian government (or editor) provide guidance that would make journalistic action ethical? How would communitarians and libertarians answer this question differently?

3. Does journalistic freedom include the right to express what one knows to be false or harmful? What do you think of Walter Lippmann's opinion that the only rationale for such freedom is to discover the truth? If you think Lippmann is wrong, how would you justify the press freedom clause of the First Amendment? What is the difference between freedom and license?

4. Since ethics is not an exact science and contains considerable subjectivity, does ethics imply the right of various journalists to do various (even conflicting) things and be considered ethical? Does freedom include the right to be unethical—or at least to be consid-

ered so by others? What would happen to the concept of press pluralism if all media followed monolithic, universal, ethical norms? If there were a unified American journalistic ethics, would this be a valuable development? Why or why not?

5. What do you think of the Enlightenment concept of a rational public? Do you believe the truth will win out in a conflict with falsehood? Can you give any examples? How long should a person have to wait for truth's victory, if it comes at all, and how would a newspaper reader, for example, know the truth if it did appear in the media? Assume the communitarian position and say why you think it is preferable to libertarianism.

References

Altschull, J. Herbert. *From Milton to McLuhan: Ideas behind American Journalism.* White Plains, NY: Longman, 1990.

Bellah, Robert N., et al. *Habits of the Heart: Individualism and Commitment in American Life.* New York: Harper & Row, 1985.

Berlin, Isaiah. *Four Essays on Liberty.* London: Oxford University Press, 1969.

Booth, Wayne. "Speech, Bought and Sold, and the 1st Amendment." *Chicago Tribune,* 1 December 1993.

Carey, George W., ed. *Freedom and Virtue.* Lanham, Md.: University Press of America, 1984.

Fromm, Erich. *Escape from Freedom.* New York: Holt, Rinehart & Winston, 1965.

Goodwin, H. Eugene. *Groping for Ethics in Journalism.* Ames: Iowa State University Press, 1983.

Hentoff, Nat. *Free Speech for Me but Not for Thee: How the American Left and Right Relentlessly Censor Each Other.* New York: HarperCollins (Perennial Library), 1993.

Kaufmann, Walter, ed. *Existentialism from Dostoevsky to Sartre.* New York: New American Library, 1975.

Lambeth, Edmund. *Committed Journalism: An Ethic for the Profession,* 2nd ed. Bloomington: Indiana University Press, 1992.

Lawler, Peter A. "Tocqueville and Revolution in His *Souvenirs.*" *The Intercollegiate Review* (spring 1991).

Levi, Albert W. "The Value of Freedom." In *Limits of Liberty: Studies of*

Mill's "On Liberty." Edited by Peter Radcliff. Belmont, Ca.: Wadsworth, 1966.

Lippmann, Walter. *The Public Philosophy.* New York: Mentor Books, 1955.

Lule, Jack. "Radical Rules: I. F. Stone's Ethical Perspective." *Journal of Mass Media Ethics*, vol. 8, no. 2 (1993).

Merrill, John C. *The Dialectic in Journalism: Toward a Responsible Use of Press Freedom.* Baton Rouge: Louisiana State University Press, 1989.

Mill, John Stuart. *On Liberty.* Edited by A. Castell. New York: Crofts, 1974.

Muller, Herbert J. *Issues of Freedom: Paradoxes and Promises.* New York: Harper & Brothers Publishers, 1960.

Nisbet, Robert A. *The Quest for Community.* New York: Oxford University Press, 1953.

Nozick, Robert. *Anarchy, State, and Utopia.* New York: Basic Books, 1974.

Radcliff, Peter, ed. *Limits of Liberty.* Belmont, Ca.: Wadsworth, 1966.

Stephen, James Fitzjames. *Liberty, Equality, Fraternity.* Edited by Stuart D. Warner. Indianapolis: Liberty Fund Press, 1993.

Sunstein, Cass. *Democracy and the Problem of Free Speech.* New York: Free Press, 1993.

Tseu, Augustinus A. *The Moral Philosophy of Mo Tzu.* Taipei: China Printing, Ltd., 1965.

von Humboldt, Wilhelm. *The Limits of State Action.* Edited by J. W. Burrow. Indianapolis: A Liberty Classics Edition, 1993.

Wilson, James Q. *The Moral Sense.* New York: Free Press, 1993.

CHAPTER FIVE

TRUTH, OBJECTIVITY, AND ETHICS

AUDIENCE MEMBER: *"Why did you use the name of my daughter in your story about the rape yesterday at the college? Don't you have any feeling for her privacy and for the embarrassment it will cause her?"*

REPORTER: *"I was just giving the truth, Mrs. Brown. Journalists are supposed to be dedicated to the truth and to full-disclosure reporting. We cannot always be worrying about the possible consequences of our stories."*

AUDIENCE MEMBER: *"But aren't you interested in being ethical?"*

REPORTER: *"Yes I am, but if I hide some important part of the story, I feel that I am being unethical."*

AUDIENCE MEMBER: *"But you can tell the truth without telling all the truth, can't you?"*

REPORTER: *"We feel we must tell all the truth we have that has been verified. I'm sorry you're upset, but I'm just doing my job."*

We now turn from the journalistic concern with the concept of freedom to perhaps the second most important journalistic concern: *truth*. In all the literature of journalism ethics, truth is the topic that probably draws the most attention. There are few journalists who do not pledge allegiance to truth; it seems to be the primary watchword of journalism and related communication activities. For instance, the "Canons of Journalism" of the American Society of Newspaper Editors (ASNE) enthrones truth and refers to "truthfulness," "accuracy," and a "clear distinction between news reports and expressions of opinion." In the *Code of Ethics* of the Society of Professional Journalists (SPJ), which is almost an exact image of the ASNE code, homage is also paid to truth, with the statements "truth is our ultimate goal," and the "duty of journalists is to serve the truth."

The SPJ code goes even further and says that journalists "must be free of obligation to any interest other than the public's right to know the truth." Truth is clearly the *sine qua non* of journalism. Almost every media group has a code of ethics exhorting members to be truthful, accurate, and objective. Perhaps the highest praise journalists can receive is that they are "dedicated to the truth."

Most news consumers in the mass communication audience expect to receive the truth, ignoring what Walter Lippmann (1965, 226) wrote years ago: "News and truth are not the same thing." Facts do not equal truth. Reporters are simply not able to get enough facts—in the proper context and with the correct balance—to tell the truth (or the whole truth) about some news event. H. Eugene Goodwin (1983, 11) gives a good example of this problem when he refers to the reporting of the Vietnam War. The journalists covering this complex and confusing war were not able to get at the truth about the war; they reported what U.S. generals said and what some troops did on a certain day. But, as Goodwin notes, these were only "facts" about the war; they were surely not the truth.

What Is Truth in Journalism?

One of the main problems with ethical codes and their deification of the truth is that they never get around to saying just what truth is. Another problem, perhaps as frustrating, is that ethical codes fail to recognize that there is often a tension—even a contradiction—between providing the truth and being ethical.

Let's look at the first issue: What is truth? Can a story be truthful if it leaves out information? If it distorts or exaggerates? If it omits the name of the source? If it quotes out of context? If it misinterprets a statement by paraphrasing it (using indirect quotations)? Does truth pertain only to what *is told* or does it also relate to what is *not* told? Is truth *all* of the truth or *some* of the truth? Is a story necessarily truthful if all the isolated facts of the story can be verified? Or, does truth go beyond the truthfulness of the facts? Can a journalist tell the truth, the whole truth, and nothing but the truth—as a courtroom witness must take an oath to do?

Most journalists agree that fabricating information violates truth-telling. And there is little doubt that no journalist can tell the whole truth. What a journalist does is provide bits and pieces of the truth. If a paraphrased version of a source's remarks does not catch the essence of what was said, then assuredly the journalist has departed from the truth. The same holds for quoting out of context. It is also the case that one does not necessarily get the truth of an event simply because all the facts that are used have been verified by the reporter.

Many journalists believe that if they give their stories a statistical underpinning, this results in truth. However, other journalists know better, and certain scientists know better as well. Many writers, including Cynthia Crossen (1994), have shown how statistics can lie. Crossen takes a skeptical look at many recent statistical studies. She points to a string of statistical sins and warns of the implied truthfulness of much of the information that floods us. The modern media consumer can just look at the wide variance in various political polls to see the impreciseness (and often outright bias) in published statistics. Perhaps, as it is with editorials, statistics take on a polemic purpose when they make their way into the stories.

A second major problem, one that goes beyond finding the truth, is the tension or even contradiction between providing the truth and being ethical. We know that a journalist often tells less than the truth *out of a basic desire to be ethical.* For example, in writing a story a reporter may refrain from giving the name of the rape victim or may eliminate gruesome or other details considered to be in "poor taste" in order to act ethically or responsibly. Truth is often intentionally compromised for the sake of ethics.

So, you may ask, what are the answers to such questions? Just what is the nature of the truth journalists are admonished to respect? Regrettably, we cannot respond to such all-encompassing questions—certainly not to anyone's satisfaction—but we can perhaps shed some light on them and at least hint at some of the answers. Students interested in learning about one of the more prominent theories of truth might want to take a look at David Weissman's *Truth's Debt to Value* (1993). For a good history of truth and a discussion of why it is a good thing in the first place, *Truth in Philosophy* by Barry Allen (1993) is an excellent source.

Accuracy: Handmaiden to Truth

Here is what one editors' group, the Associated Press Managing Editors, has proposed for its ethics code in regard to accuracy: "Newspapers should develop and use safeguards to avoid error. These should include systematic verification of facts and quotations and corroboration of critical information" (Shepard, 1994, 40). This statement is typical of the emphasis journalists put on accuracy in the media. Journalistic rhetoric is filled with exhortations for increased accuracy.

Accuracy for a journalist is very important, of course, but accuracy (getting the exact facts and figures and spelling names correctly) does not equal truth, which is a much bigger concept. Accuracy adds to truth, is a part of truth, and is extremely important in journalism in that it is a rather easily detectable aspect of truthful reporting. Inaccuracies lead to a lessening of credibility for the media. People should be quoted accurately, names should be spelled correctly, addresses should be given precisely, and facts and statistics should be reported accurately. Yet careful readers know that media provide many inaccurate stories—meaning that parts of the stories contain inaccuracies.

Let us look for a moment at newspapers. They, especially, seem to be in a quandary as they try to decide which mistakes to correct and how prominently to display the corrections. Some editors think it is healthy for a paper to admit errors and see the running of corrections as an effort to build credibility with the public. Others believe that a publication can harm itself by admitting mistakes, even errors of a trivial nature. Credibility can actually be harmed, they say, by publishing a list of corrections. Other editors think that only big mistakes— not small ones like misspelling a name—should be admitted, even if they are not apologized for.

Henry McNulty, the reader representative (ombudsman) for the *Hartford Courant*, has said that "accuracy, corrections and clarifications are all part of newspaper managers' thinking more about readers" (Rykken, 1991, 6). The *Courant* is one newspaper that corrects errors with almost religious fervor, publishing about a hundred corrections a month. His paper, McNulty says, is "very picky, down to the middle initials" in its stories. "If we say so-and-so is the 12th commissioner and he is the 11th, we'll correct it."

Some editors even believe that there is merit in telling the readers in a correction exactly who on the staff made the error. Thomas Winship, retired editor of the *Boston Globe*, is one who believes this and he gives the following reason: "The integrity of newspapers is on the line today" and "We've got to do everything humanly possible to recapture our readership and the confidence people have in their newspapers" (Rykken, 6).

Not all journalists would agree. For example, Susan Miller, Scripps Howard Newspapers' vice president/editorial, sees no reason for what she calls "public humiliation" in publishing the names of error makers. She believes that editors should not be "punitive" but should look for "patterns of errors and ways to correct them" (10).

Today, with computer databases of all kinds, journalists have an added opportunity to be accurate. Databases of street names and elected officials' names are commonly used in newsrooms for checking copy. Software to correct misspelled words is also available on editorial computer systems. This electronic help is important, but most of the responsibility for accuracy falls squarely on the reporters who get and write the stories and on the copyeditors who edit them. Perhaps as many as a hundred newspapers, like the *Ledger* of Lakeland, Florida, make phone calls to ten people a week quoted in stories as a check on accuracy. Many papers that perform accuracy checks do so by writing to sources and including copies of relevant stories. At least one newspaper, the *Columbia Missourian*, the teaching daily paper of the University of Missouri School of Journalism, routinely checks facts with sources quoted in stories *before* publication, a procedure used years before by such magazines as *The New Yorker* and *Time*.

Some newspapers attempt to appraise their accuracy on the basis of the corrections they run, comparing them with other publications. Researchers believe that this is a poor method. For example, Philip E. Meyer, professor of journalism at the University of North Carolina, says that papers that give more attention to correcting errors will receive more corrections from readers, while those that publish few corrections will hear less often from readers. Therefore, Meyer says, such comparison measurement is not a valid indicator of a newspaper's error rate (Rykken, 1991, 8).

Meyer does, however, advocate that newspapers audit themselves for accuracy, as accountants do with their corpora-

Truth, Objectivity, and Ethics

tion's financial records. In 1986 he proposed such a practice. "Neither fairness nor balance nor objectivity means much if the facts are not right," he wrote in a paper published by the Gannett Center for Media Studies (now the Freedom Forum Media Studies Center) in New York City. Such an auditing system was pioneered as far back as 1936 by the University of Minnesota as a means of checking the accuracy of the campus newspaper. In writing about the Meyer proposal, Tom Collins (1986, 4) of *Newsday* said rather skeptically that such audits would, he supposed, demonstrate "how credible and ethical the newspaper is." Collins, like many journalists, has serious doubts about the wisdom of doing such audits and believes that an "accuracy audit sounds more like an inaccuracy audit."

Collins notes that Meyer keeps "throwing the First Amendment up at the press, his argument being that 'without accuracy in reporting, First Amendment claims are empty.' It has an intimidating ring to it until you remember that the First Amendment doesn't mention anything about newspapers having to be accurate, or for that matter, responsible" (4).

Accuracy Checking: A Slow Trend

Despite the perspective given by Collins, most editors are at least amenable to accuracy checks or audits. They can "throw useful light on how the subjects of news stories perceive their coverage," says Gilbert Cranberg (1987, 15). "Accuracy checks are worthless if they tell news organizations simply what somebody thinks they want to hear. Worse, the checks may lull the press into a false sense of security."

Often it is difficult to do accuracy checks because of the isolation and defensiveness of sources. Howard Kurtz (1993, 34) provides an example of a big media conglomerate itself refusing to give out information to the press. Al Neuharth, chairman of the Gannett's Freedom Forum Foundation, refused to be interviewed in 1993 about a New York attorney

111

general's probe into whether the tax-exempt foundation was spending too much on perks and overhead. Reporter Anne Lowrey Bailey, of the *Chronicle of Philanthropy*, said that the foundation (dedicated to promoting "free press, free speech, and free spirit") rejected five written requests to talk to Neuharth or foundation president Charles Overby and would not answer most of her written questions.

Are some stories simply too good to check out for accuracy? Kurtz (1993, 34) also tells of the *New York Post's* gruesome report of a man who allegedly raped a three-year-old girl near a crowded Manhattan highway while motorists stopped to watch. The paper's banner headline proclaimed: "Shame on the City—Shocking Story of New York at Its Worst." The article described the incident as "a chilling mix of apathy and voyeurism." But the story was not true. It turned out that three motorists had helped pursue the alleged rapist, and traffic had stalled behind their abandoned cars. The *Post*, however, never ran a follow-up story setting the record straight.

The relationship of such inaccurate stories to ethics is obvious. Journalists' avoidance of accurate reporting regularly draws criticism from media watchers, journalism reviews, and media watchdog groups such as Accuracy in Media (AIM). Emerging in 1984, AIM tried to fill the vacuum that was created by the demise of the National News Council. Reed Irvine founded and heads AIM, an organization that watches the media from a conservative perspective and points out inaccuracies on a regular basis. Although Irvine has his detractors as well as supporters, he is persistent in trying to purge the press of what he perceives to be its unethical and arrogant behavior. Several other groups (such as FAIR, the liberal counterpart of AIM), are doing virtually the same thing.

Ben J. Wattenberg, of the American Enterprise Institute for Public Policy Research, in referring to AIM, has said: "Generally speaking, it is healthy that it [the press] is observed, scrutinized and criticized from all spots on the spectrum. AIM is one of the players in that game. They have every right to do what they do, and it is probably useful" (Bonafede, 1986, 112). Media critic Edwin Diamond, quoted in the same article, said that he sees worthwhile benefits flowing from AIM's media watch. "I'm one of those who believes there is a need for such criticism and letting a thousand flowers bloom," Diamond says. "The more people telling the press to pull up their socks the better."

Accuracy, as we have said, is one aspect of truth, and the seeking of truth is a prominent journalistic ethical imperative. It might be well for us to consider the concept of truth a little more in depth. Let us analyze further this complex topic.

Analyzing Truth: Its Levels and Ethics

One reason journalists and others have so much trouble with "the truth" is that they are never quite sure just what kind of truth they're dealing with. Or, said another way, they don't take into consideration what has been referred to as the *levels* of truth (Merrill, Lee, and Friedlander, 1994, ch. 2). One must remember that, as the general semanticists say, truth-1 is not truth-2; there are different kinds of truth, and a person must be clear about which type is being alluded to (see Figure 5-1).

At least five levels of truth can be examined. Three of them are clearly within the purview of the journalist, and two of them are really beyond the scope of journalistic enquiry. Let us look briefly at the five levels.

> Level 1: *Transcendental truth.* This is Truth with a capital "T." The journalist cannot ascend to this level; it is beyond the journalist and all of us. It is the all-encompassing Truth, the complete, overshadowing Truth, the Truth that goes beyond the potential grasp of a human being. It is Truth in its totality. And naturally, it cannot be found or communicated.

FIGURE 5-1
LEVELS OF TRUTH

TRANSCENDENTAL
Total Truth—Truth with a Capital "T"

POTENTIAL
What the Journalist *Can Get*

SELECTED
What the Journalist *Does Get*

↓

REPORTED
What the Journalist *Uses*

AUDIENCE-PERCEIVED TRUTH
What the Audience Members Select and Ingest from the
Reported Truth

Level 2: *Potential truth.* This truth is composed of the aspects of
Transcendental truth that can possibly be grasped by human perception, research, and rationality. The journalist
can, if diligent and persistent enough, obtain potential
truth—or portions of it—for inclusion in a story. This level,
although it is never reached completely by the journalist,
can serve as an ideal or goal.

Level 3: *Selected truth.* This is the part of the potential truth
that is actually abstracted or selected from the total reality

of the story by the journalist. It is the portion of the truth that the journalist has managed to perceive, or to get into notes, tape, or film. It is thus the raw material for the story.

Level 4: *Reported truth.* This is the part of the selected truth that the journalist actually reports. It is certainly only part of the accumulated data that the journalist has perceived or has as raw material. Undoubtedly, it is the most important part of the truth in that it is the part (or level) that represents, or gives an image of, an event in reality. It is certainly the part of the truth that the journalist can control. The better the reporter, the more of the truth he or she will report.

Level 5: *Audience-perceived truth.* This is perhaps the lowest level of truth—at least the lowest in the sense of being the final step in the process of message entropy (loss of information from the message during the process of creation and transmission). The journalist has absolutely no control over this level. The reporter reports, and the audience member perceives the report or portions of it. The reporter has no control over the amount of truth finally getting to the brain of the receiver.

We can see that the journalist has nothing to say about the first and fifth levels of truth. The first, Transcendental truth, eludes the journalist and everybody else, and the fifth level, audience-perceived truth, is likewise beyond the control of the reporter. We can say, then, that truth is always limited. The care and zealousness of reporters at the third level have much to do with the amount of truth left at the fourth level. And although journalists cannot control the amount of truth perceived by the audience at the fifth level, they can determine the thoroughness of truth at the fourth level.

After looking at these levels of truth, we might wonder just what they have to do with journalistic ethics. In fact, these levels have a great deal to do with ethics. The determination or will to reach the maximum levels of journalistic truth (the third and fourth levels) theoretically permeates the activities of the journalist and provides a motivation or foundation for ethical reporting. Not necessarily being truthful but having a *desire* to be truthful is the underpinning of ethical journalism. As Walter Lippmann (1955) wrote, the reason for having freedom of expression is that truth might be discovered. Thus, it should not be difficult to connect truth, freedom, and ethics. If journalists are ethical, they will use freedom to discover the truth. Freedom not used for unearthing the truth will thus be suspect from an ethical perspective.

Lippmann goes on to say that genuine debate is useful for getting at the truth, but merely expressing oneself freely about any subject does not advance the truth. Freedom must be rooted in advancing the truth. According to Lippmann (1955, 100), when debate is lacking, "freedom of speech does not work as it is meant to work. It has lost the principle which regulates it and justifies it—that is to say, dialectic conducted according to logic and the rules of evidence." If there is no underlying desire for the truth and no effective debate, then "the unrestricted right to speak will unloose so many propagandists, procurers, and panderers upon the public that sooner or later in self-defense the people will turn to the censors to protect them."

Mahatma Gandhi, the great Indian religious leader and social philosopher, had no doubt that truth and ethics are inseparable. He puts the utmost emphasis on truthfulness (*satya*), one of the cardinal virtues (Datta, 1953, 94–95). For Gandhi, truthfulness basically means "a devotion to facts and eagerness to discover the truth of any matter." How would Gandhi propose that we discover the truth? By careful observation, by listing evidence, and by the dispassionate use of reason. In addition, the discovery of truth requires self-analysis and self-purification. Gandhi would say that journalists cannot find the truth and report it if they are angry, lustful, greedy, or prideful; he would insist that only a person who is morally strong can find the truth—especially in social and political controversies. Therefore, Gandhi would say that the unethical journalist who thinks he or she can provide truthful reports is mistaken. The foundation of ethics, for Gandhi, is truth.

Objectivity in Journalism

Objectivity, another concept in journalism, is related to both truth and accuracy. The Society of Professional Journalists' *Code of Ethics* (1987) says: "Truth is our ultimate goal." But the *Code* proceeds to say that "objectivity in reporting the news is another goal." The code writers evidently see truth and objectivity as different things. Many journalists would consider truth, accuracy, and objectivity all part of the same concept, with the last two being subsumed by the first. It is a fuzzy area, however, and the case could be made that truthful journalism is actually part of journalistic objectivity. In any event, accuracy in journalism is related closely to truth and to objectivity.

Journalistic objectivity connotes a relationship between symbol and reality, with virtual correspondence of meaning, or harmonizing, being the result. Objectivity can, semantically, conjure up completeness of knowledge, or it may suggest natural informational limitations kept to a minimum by the attitude of the communicator. When journalists consider the broader aspects of ethics, they must be concerned with the spread of knowledge. They should want that knowledge (their stories) to be as thorough and as accurate as possible, to conform maximally to reality.

Not only facts—but *meanings*—enter into the concept of objective journalism. *Epistemology* (the science of knowledge) and *semantics* (the study of meaning) have a symbiotic or integrated relationship. Knowledge is impossible without meaning,

117

and meaning is extremely complex—and certainly relative. If we don't know what some message means, we cannot derive knowledge from it. In short, we cannot *know*. If journalists want to impart truth, they must be concerned with both epistemology and semantics. They must get the real facts, the real story, and as much of the story as possible. They must then present these facts in a meaningful context that approximates the event in reality.

Of course, as Neil Postman (1986, 17) has pointed out, the whole concept of truth (and of epistemology generally) is an "opaque subject," and its definitions are derived, "at least in part, from the character of the media of communication through which information is conveyed." Having a media technological perspective similar to McLuhan, Postman maintains that truth is a kind of cultural prejudice (23), related closely to the medium under consideration. Writing, he says, gets at truth better than does television, and it has a healthier influence on the cultures that adopt it. He believes (24) that the decline of a print-based epistemology and the rise of a television epistemology have "had grave consequences for public life," and that "we are getting sillier by the minute."

Being truthful should be the reporter's general or normal goal, regardless of the epistemological difficulties. It is certainly an ethical imperative for the journalist. This is the case even though, on occasion, the journalist may feel an ethical urge to depart from the truth, as we will discuss in Chapter 8. At this point we can say that a journalist must have a deep respect for truth and its close relative, objectivity. All conscientious journalists should, as the SPJ *Code of Ethics* recommends, consider their allegiance to the truth and their duty to serve it. Serving the truth brings up frustrating semantic problems both with the concept of "serving" the truth and with the concept of "truth" itself. But it is the urge, the desire, the will to be truthful that is important; it might be well to remember this as we proceed now into some rather dense semantic thickets.

Objectivity As Myth and As Ideal

What is objective journalism? Is it a realizable goal, or does it simply serve as an ideal toward which to strive? For the sake of simplifying our discussion, let us propose that there are two principal ways of looking at journalistic objectivity:

1. As a "myth," purely and simply—an impossible goal to achieve
2. As a largely reachable ideal or goal, which forces the journalist to try to be fair, accurate, thorough, balanced, dispassionate, uninvolved, unbiased, and unprejudiced

It may be interesting to contemplate the first view of objectivity, but the notion of "myth" negates the meaning of the term if we look at objectivity as a story that perfectly reflects the reality and fullness of the actual event. However well "an impossible goal" reflects the principle that one cannot say everything about anything, it denies the evidence of our critical senses and judgment. In other words, it denies that there really *is* a difference between a story that can be considered basically objective and one that can be considered mostly subjective.

The second of these views of objectivity is the more traditional one and is generally accepted in journalistic circles. It is based on the assumption that journalists can, to a significant extent, objectify their stories by demanding of themselves as much thoroughness, accuracy, and balance (correspondence to reality) as is humanly possible. What is stressed here is that the reporter's *attitude* basically determines objectivity.

When people use such terms as *objective reporter* or *objective journalism,* they are speaking of a diligent attempt to convey reality in words or pictures. They are talking about effort and *degree.* The term *objectivity* has come to mean disinterested, fair, and balanced. Obviously, it is impossible to be objective in the sense of relaying to the audience the totality or

119

fullness of reality or the actual event. One must admit that a reporter, trapped in the inadequacy of language and personal psychological and ideological conditioning, cannot perfectly objectify anything in communication. Reporters strain reality through their perceptual filters, and it always comes out with some distortion.

In a sense, then, the anti-objectivists are correct. It should be noted, however, that those who contend that a journalist *can* be objective are not thinking in absolutes. They are saying that a journalist with a proper *attitude* and one who is diligent and persistent can go very far along the objectivity continuum. Some journalists may think that they can really be objective, but they are undoubtedly defining the term in the relativistic sense just noted. The Society of Professional Journalists, for instance, says in its *Code* (1987) that objectivity "serves as the mark of an experienced professional" and that "it is a standard of performance toward which we strive." But then the *Code* proceeds to imply that objectivity can actually be reached, by stating that "we honor those who achieve it." Certainly objectivity is a necessary aspect of ethical journalism, as the SPJ *Code* emphasizes.

Perhaps the most rational way to conceive of objectivity is to think of it as a goal or an ideal toward which to strive, knowing, of course, that it can never be reached. For the journalist, this is similar to the first and highest level of truth, the Transcendental level. Such an objectivity does indeed exist— out there in reality—but it cannot be trapped or captured in its fullness by even the most perceptive and diligent reporter. As an ideal, it is useful to the conscientious journalist who aspires to get as close to it as possible.

Another way to think of objectivity is the way Erich Fromm (1966, 111) does. He says that objectivity requires more than mere accuracy; it requires that the observer become related in some way to that which is being reported. He goes on to say: "Objectivity is not, as it is often implied in a false idea of 'scientific' objectivity, synonymous with detachment, with absence of interest and care. How can one penetrate the veiling surface of things to their causes and relationships if one does not have an interest that is vital and sufficiently impelling for so laborious a task?"

Fromm is not identifying objectivity with detachment or neutrality, as many journalists would. Rather, he is saying that objectivity has more to do with respect. He stresses the idea that lack of interest as a condition for recognizing the truth is fallacious. For Fromm, all productive thinking, observing, and communicating are driven by the observer's interest and respect for the essence of what is being observed and reported. Fromm's perspective, which is shared by many (including most existentialists) highlights another view of objectivity: that the reporter's subjective values and interpretations are vital to any concept of objective reporting.

Assumptions Related to Objectivity

Several false assumptions must be taken into consideration when we talk of objective reporting. The first is that journalists are *free* to be (or to try to be) objective. No reporters, even in libertarian societies, are ever entirely free because of their conditioning by experience, intelligence, circumstances, environment, education, biases, and a host of other factors. Reporters are, in effect, conditioned to be *non*objective.

A second assumption is that journalists can be objective in the sense of being able to present the whole story. This, too, is false. All reporters *must* be selective, and this selectivity involves being *subjective*—selecting and using information that fits their existing ideas as to what constitutes news. It is obvious that a journalist selects, and this selection of what goes into the story (or the selection of the story itself) automatically subjectivizes it, in a real sense biasing and distorting the reality that the journalist is trying to objectify.

121

A third assumption is that journalists can be *detached.* Any reporter trying to get at the meaning of the story must become involved—making judgments and taking positions with regard to the persons and perspectives given in the story. Even if true detachment were possible, it is doubtful that it would assure objectivity. Subjectivists, in fact, insist that the value given to detachment is in itself a sign of subjectivity.

Then there is a fourth assumption—that journalists can be *unprejudiced.* Prejudice, like many of these other terms, is difficult to define, but it is usually understood to mean a preconceived opinion for or against something held without adequate reason. The key word is *adequate.* Is not all reporting, ask the subjectivists, based on at least some degree of prejudice, or inconclusive evidence? Can you imagine reporters operating in a context in which they would have no prejudices? The more complex and controversial the reportorial context, the more prejudice becomes operative.

A fifth assumption is that reporters can keep personal opinions out of their stories. But, it may be asked, how can reporters select certain things to include, or what emphasis to give them, without acting on their opinions? In fact, how can an editor or reporter decide to cover a particular event in the first place without acting on opinions? Journalistic opinions determine the entire editorial decision-making process, say the subjectivists, and when journalists express opinions, they are being subjective.

A sixth assumption is that if journalists are detached and unbiased, they can present events that are balanced and undistorted. A photograph, many would say, is true to the subject and thus balanced, unbiased, and undistorted—in short, objective. But pictures can lie, and they often distort reality. In a study of cameramen, Elisabeth Noelle-Neumann (1984), a German public opinion scholar, found that cameramen admitted that they would take eye-level pictures of national leaders they personally liked and pictures "from above" of those they did not like, thus making them look stupid. It is also obvious that a photographer taking a picture (or representation) of a building, for instance, can provide a picture that is favorable or one that is unfavorable simply by taking the picture from a certain perspective—for example, by focusing on it from a trashy parking lot or by approaching it from an aesthetically pleasing angle.

Armand Mattelart (1980, 39), a French sociologist who questions journalistic objectivity, says that the concept forms "the golden rule of journalistic practice, the cornerstone of its professional deontology, and the equivalent of the Hippocratic oath." However, he does not believe such objectivity exists. Why? First, he says, the concept presupposes that certain journalistic perceptive powers are capable of penetrating reality. Second, he thinks the concept postulates that the mere presentation of facts (purporting to be what they are *in themselves* and not what the journalist sees them to be) goes no further than the facts themselves. Finally, Mattelart says that facts are *isolated* by objectivity-oriented journalism—"cut off from their roots, deprived of the conditions which would explain their occurrence and detached from the social system which endows them with meaning and in which they possess an intelligible place."

Stephanie Gutmann (1993, 55) mentions the "cult of objectivity" as one source of the media's current problems. "There is just one problem with this: objectivity is impossible," she contends. She contrasts objectivity with fairness "in which a writer takes account of his own biases and attempts to control for them."

Gutmann goes on to compare writing to furnishing a room: a series of choices. She quotes Carl Bernstein as saying that reporting "is not stenography." All writers can do, Gutmann says, is *select* the anecdotes, facts, images, and opinions they think best convey the truth, and that, of course, subjectivizes the stories. In television, the same highly selective content is operable because the reporters are choosing and ordering the shots to be shown. At the root of all disclaimers to objective reporting is this business of selection.

Objectivists see the frequent use of fiction in reports as playing too loosely with the truth. The popular book, *The Agenda: Inside the Clinton White House*, written by journalist Bob Woodward (1994) highlights the ethical problems connected with trying to treat fact as fiction. The Woodward technique represents a genre (a fallout from the "new journalism" of the 1960s) that increasingly is being used in journalism. There is a lack of documentation (footnotes or source identification) in the Woodward book about the Clintons, and this casts doubts on its veracity. At any rate, as James Atlas (1994, E–5) points out, we'll never know whether or not Woodward has told the truth about the chaos at the White House—or at least not for a long, long time, since the research materials have been deposited in the library at Yale and sealed for forty years.

Truth: The Foundation of Journalism Ethics

In journalism, the ideal is to be as truthful as possible. The story should maximize reality and should provide documentation, including the sources of quotations. Even though, from time to time, a journalist might *intentionally* be less than objective or truthful (such as not revealing sources) in order to be *more* ethical, a sound ethics normally would involve accuracy and a dedication to truth-telling. Most philosophers, while favoring truthfulness and bemoaning secrecy, recognize that exceptions must be made on occasion. For the most part, these exceptions are made by conscientious journalists trying to be ethical.

Sissela Bok (1978) notes that journalists will often not fabricate outright, but they will ignore certain aspects of a story which would add to its total truth (see box, p. 125). According

Sissela Bok (1930–)

Sissela Bok is a modern philosopher who has written much on the subject of truth, lying, and ethics in general. Many of her writings are of direct importance to the journalist. The daughter of Gunnar and Alva Myrdal, she was born in Stockholm, Sweden, and became an American citizen in 1959. She was educated at the Sorbonne, at Washington University, and at Harvard.

Dr. Bok has taught and lectured in philosophy at several universities and colleges and has served on many boards and committees concerned with medical ethics. She is a fellow and member of the board of the Hastings Institute of Society, Ethics, and Life Sciences and is also a fellow of the Institute for Philosophy and Religion of Boston University.

She is best known for her *Lying: Moral Choice in Public and Private Life* (1979) and *Secrets: On the Ethics of Concealment and Revelation* (1982), both of which deal with the ethics of journalism. *Lying* gives much attention to the ramifications of journalistic lying. Bok differs from other philosophers (especially Kant) in thinking that lying is often justified. When one can avoid harm in special situations, she believes, this avoidance can take precedence over the principle of truthfulness. Other topics dealt with in *Lying* include using silence, avoiding subjects alto-

to Bok, this is neither ethical nor a sign of good professional reporting. Bok stresses the principle that a journalist should be a truth-teller, but she does say that occasionally, in very special situations, lying is justified. She does not tell us when it might be so justified in journalism, but presumably it would be in cases such as not revealing the name of a rape victim or not identifying some source who might be harmed if named in the

continued

gether, and telling harmless (little "white") lies. Often, for instance, journalists will not fabricate outright, but they will ignore certain parts of a story which would add to its total truth. Generally this is not ethical, according to Bok, and it certainly is not good professional reporting.

Bok's 1982 book, *Secrets*, gives attention to journalists' reportorial problems, especially the dialectical clash between concealment and exposure, and between the people's right to know and the right of privacy. Bok thinks that journalists should probe and expose secrecy in commercial and governmental circles. They should be motivated to counterbalance the deep-seated secrecy found in public institutions. The press, she contends, is free to try to unearth information about the institutions of society (about government, especially). However, it is constantly hampered by claims of confidentiality and by the natural inclination of institutions to keep secrets.

Bok concludes her insightful and wise words for the journalist with this observation from *Secrets*: "Because the task of reporting the news is both an indispensable public resource and big business, and because of the great power now wielded by the media, a commitment to openness and to accountability is more necessary than ever."

story. Bok seems to believe that when a journalist can avoid harm in special situations, this avoidance can override the principle of truthfulness. In this sense, she parts company with philosophers like Immanuel Kant, whose stern legalistic ethics would broach no exception to truth-telling.

It is safe to say that truth-telling and journalistic objectivity, vague as they may be on close analysis, together may serve as a moral foundation for journalistic ethics. Regardless of what aspects of ethics we may encounter in this book, the concept of truth-telling will always rise up and demand to be dealt with. When journalists depart from the fullest truth possible in a story—even for the most *ethical* reasons—such an action probably leaves a certain uneasiness that never quite goes away. The ethics of truth-telling in journalism, like other ethical problems, will probably never be resolved to everyone's satisfaction. But in this chapter we have taken the first step across the threshold of journalistic ethics: We have encountered and considered the spirit of truth that undergirds the entire practice of journalism.

ANALYZING ETHICAL ISSUES

1. The SPJ *Code of Ethics* says that journalists "must be free of obligation to any interest other than the public's right to know the truth." If that is the case, why was there a need to put many other "interests" into the *Code?* Where does the public get a right to know the truth? Do you think that truth is the ultimate goal of journalism? Does press freedom not provide the right for a journalist to tell less than the truth? Do journalists even *try* to tell the truth in their stories?

2. Is truth often compromised in journalism for the sake of ethics? If you think so, can you give any examples? If truth is the highest good in journalism, then perhaps you should be studying epistemology (the science of knowledge) rather than ethics. What do you think about that? How would you respond to such an implication? When audience members get a variety of "truths" from the press about a certain event, how are they to know what to believe?

3. Can a story be truthful if it is not accurate? Can a story be accurate but not truthful? Is truth in reporting necessarily correlated to

127

credibility? If a newspaper is not truthful, can its readers believe it and have faith in it? Why do many newspapers have "accuracy checks" but no "truth checks"?

4. Is journalistic objectivity possible? Why would the SPJ *Code* call it the journalist's goal and say that "we honor those who achieve it"? What are some of the main meanings of objectivity? What do you think of Habermas's saying that although objectivity is not possible, what is needed is "the ideal of reliable information" and that without this ideal "everything is lost"?

5. Do you agree with Sissela Bok that it is unethical for a journalist to ignore certain aspects of a story? Why would she say that a journalist should be a truth-teller and at the same time say that, on occasion, lying is justified? Which is more possible—being a truth-teller or a truth-seeker? If a journalist is to be ethical, should she try to put all the truth that she has sought (and found) into her story?

References

Allen, Barry. *Truth in Philosophy.* Cambridge: Harvard University Press, 1993.

Atlas, James. "When Fact Is Treated as Fiction." *New York Times,* 24 July 1994.

Bok, Sissela. *Lying: Moral Choice in Public and Private Life.* New York: Vintage Books, 1979.

Bonafede, Dom. "One Man's Accuracy." *National Journal,* 20 May 1986.

Collins, Tom. "Accuracy Audits: A Really Bad Idea for the Press." *Publishers' Auxiliary,* vol. 122, no. 10, 19 May 1986.

Cranberg, Gilbert. "Credibility: Accuracy Checks." *ASNE Bulletin* (July–August 1987).

Crossen, Cynthia. *Tainted Truth: The Manipulation of Fact in America.* New York: Simon & Schuster, 1994.

Datta, Dhirendra M. *The Philosophy of Mahatma Gandhi.* Madison: University of Wisconsin Press, 1953.

Fromm, Erich. *Man for Himself.* New York: Fawcett, 1966.

Goodwin, H. Eugene. *Groping for Ethics in Journalism.* Ames: Iowa State University Press, 1983.

Truth, Objectivity, and Ethics

Gutmann, Stephanie. "The Breeding Ground." *National Review*, 21 June 1993.

Kurtz, Howard. "Why the Press Is Always Right." *Columbia Journalism Review* (May–June 1993).

Lippmann, Walter. *Public Opinion*. New York: Free Press, 1965.

———. *The Public Philosophy*. New York: Mentor Books, 1955.

Mattelart, Armand. *Mass Media, Ideologies, and the Revolutionary Movement*. Atlantic Highlands, NJ: Humanities Press, 1980.

Merrill, John C., John Lee, and E. Jay Friedlander. *Modern Mass Media*, 2nd ed. New York: HarperCollins, 1994.

Noelle-Neumann, Elisabeth. *The Spiral of Silence: Public Opinion, Our Social Skin*. Chicago: University of Chicago Press, 1984.

Postman, Neil. *Amusing Ourselves to Death*. New York: Penguin Books, 1986.

Rykken, Rolf. "New Tactics Mark the Push of Accuracy." *Presstime* (July 1991).

Shepard, Alicia C. "Legislating Ethics." *American Journalism Review* (January–February 1994).

Society of Professional Journalists. *Code of Ethics*. 1987.

Weissman, David. *Truth's Debt to Value*. New Haven: Yale University Press, 1993.

Woodward, Bob. *The Agenda: Inside the Clinton White House*. Hingham, Mass.: Wheeler Publishing, Inc., 1994.

CHAPTER SIX

PROPAGANDA: RETREAT FROM ETHICS

Propaganda is the dark side of journalism, the slippery slope on which journalists easily lose their ethical footing and fall headlong into the slough of self-aggrandizement. No journalist, of course, admits to being a propagandist. However, in a profession of strongminded, opinionated people, it is natural that there is a tendency to try to persuade, to spread various values, and to precipitate action. The journalist who reports on troubles in such places as the Balkans, Rwanda, Israel and the new Palestinian territories, or the Korean peninsula will find it difficult to report without expressing a hidden agenda—submerged biases, a desire for certain outcomes, sympathy for one side, and so forth. Propaganda, we may conclude, is generally antagonistic to ethical journalism since it is infused with deception and selfish motivation. Ethical journalism, in contrast, springs from a sense of altruism and public responsibility.

Let us turn now to propaganda, which lures many journalists away from a concern for ethics. We can see how propaganda intrudes into the moral fabric of journalism and attracts journalists with its alluring assurances of success and power, and its skillful manipulation of people and situations. By using propaganda, journalists may believe they can achieve their personal goals and may rationalize that good ends justify any means

(Machiavellianism). Certainly we do not want to paint this picture with too broad a brush. It may be that propagandistic journalists are the exception, but there is little doubt that many of them exist.

We should realize at the start that journalists have the constitutional right to be propagandists. Peter Stoler (1986, 196) put it this way: "The First Amendment . . . does not really say much about the press at all. It does not say that it must be responsible, or fair, or honest. . . . All the First Amendment says is that the press must be free, which means that it is free to ask questions and to publish whatever it can learn." This fact, of course, opens wide the door to the unethical journalist, just as it opens the door to the ethical journalist.

No journalist wants to be considered a propagandist. The term has a bad connotation. This does not mean that no journalist wants *to be* a propagandist. In fact, part of propagandizing is managing to keep others from recognizing propagandists for what they are. Journalists generally wish to avoid being considered people who do not play fair with the audience, who are not honest, and who are pulling the proverbial wool over someone's eyes. It is true that the journalists who are propagandists may be only "a few bad apples" but, as the old saying goes, they can ruin the journalistic "barrel."

As was discussed in Chapter 5, the ethical journalist is dedicated to truth, objectivity, and fairness. Thus, when a journalist slips into the mode of propaganda, there has been a retreat from ethics. The journalist repudiates ethical concern and sets aside such principles as truthfulness, fairness, and the companion virtue of being forthright with the audience.

Journalists make much noise about the propaganda that exists in government, big business, and other social constituencies (such as various religious groups, labor unions, environmental groups, and political factions such as conservatives and liberals). Ever anxious to point out propaganda in others, the media people are not so serious when it comes to noting and correcting their own propagandistic tendencies. Because journalists consider themselves honest brokers for the public, persons who are in the business of telling the truth with no axes to grind, they are often blind to their own lapses as they slip into propagandizing.

Propaganda: Its Basic Nature

Many journalists might quarrel with what has just been said, contending that they are really not propagandists and that the trouble comes from a loose definition of the term. What they would likely contend is that government spokespersons, for example, are propagandists when they keep some information from the press, but journalists are *not* propagandists when they keep a story (or parts of it) from the audience. Journalists might also insist that they have no ulterior motives for leaving out stories or parts of them. Of course, government officials can say the same thing about their message-control activities. This whole subject of propaganda in journalism is not a popular one (at least with journalists), but it is an important one. Journalists who are propagandists are, by and large, unethical, and that is justification enough for the subject to be dealt with here.

A General Meaning of Propaganda

It is difficult to define *propaganda* in a precise and meaningful way, and we shall get to that presently. First, though, let us consider the usual connotative (or "lay") meanings of the term *propaganda* and its importance to journalism. Its general connotation is: purposely less than honest, deceptive, biased, irrational, exaggerated or simplistic, secretive, success oriented, and devoid of a sense of fairness. Is this general connotation important in journalism? Of course it is. For the very nature of news reporting is almost the opposite: It is to be as truthful and objective (accurate, thorough, balanced, and fair) as is humanly possible.

One kind of information dissemination that is in the twilight zone between intentional and unintentional propaganda is what is known as *disinformation.* Television, especially, is a purveyer of disinformation, or what Neil Postman (1986, 107) calls "misleading information—misplaced, irrelevant, fragmented or superficial information." According to Postman, this is information that "creates the illusion of knowing something but which in fact leads one away from knowing." In stressing the disinformational proclivity of television, Postman states:

> I do not mean to imply that television news deliberately
> aims to deprive Americans of a coherent, contextual un-
> derstanding of their world. I mean to say that when
> news is packaged as entertainment, that is the inevitable
> result. . . . I am saying we are losing our sense of what
> it means to be well informed. Ignorance is always correct-
> able. But what shall we do if we take ignorance to be
> knowledge (107–8)?

Is it unethical, then, to stress entertainment instead of news? It may well be, since such a substitution is usually done with the knowledge that it is depriving the audience of serious and needed information. We are contending in this chapter that journalists can be far more ethical than they are if they recognize the lure of propaganda (and its cousin, disinformation) and determine not to embrace it. We maintain that to be propagandistic is to be unethical. We realize, at the same time, that many people give such a broad definition to the term that it becomes almost meaningless. For example, some say that to "propagate" is to spread or convey information and that therefore the very business of journalism is to propagate or propagandize. (It should be noted that the origin of the term *propaganda* began with the Roman Catholic Church in 1622, when it set up the *sacra congregatio de propaganda fide,* the branch of the Church specifically concerned with the propagation of the faith.)

When propaganda becomes synonymous with the organized dissemination of messages, it loses any kind of journalistic meaning. Propaganda in the context of journalism, or the context of the mass media, must be something more limited, more specific, and more distinct. For our purpose, journalistic propaganda will be considered those messages purposely designed to diminish the reliability, objectivity, balance, and thoroughness of journalism.

At this point, an obvious journalistic objection will be raised. What about editorial writers and so-called interpretive or analytical writers and speakers who regularly use propaganda techniques to help them achieve their persuasive purposes? This is a reasonable objection, and many would affirm that such propagandistic journalism in the *non-news* areas of journalism is appropriate (or allowable) and is not unethical. The straight newscast on radio and television or the news story in the press may be the only journalistic areas still paying lip service to the evils of propaganda. Even here, as we shall see later, propaganda works its way into the very substance of news reporting.

Propaganda today is spilling over into all areas of journalism, not only in advertising—where one would expect it—but in voice inflections in radio and television, facial expressions, stories, headlines, photographs, and captions. It is difficult to verify the spread of propaganda, but one's common sense and sensitivity to word and action make its presence rather obvious. We can see it in what the media choose to emphasize and in what they choose to play down or to ignore. Is this simply news judgment? Many observers would say that the process of journalistic agenda setting is itself a propaganda device. Some cynics would even suggest that journalism *is* propaganda. Such beliefs are extreme, but we think that journalists who are concerned with being ethical will want to eliminate as much propaganda as possible. The distinction between propaganda and nonpropaganda must be preserved in journalism; it must be recognized that some journalism is properly propagandistic and other journalism is not.

Some Defining Characteristics

When journalists consider propaganda in journalism, they must look directly at many of the first principles of journalistic endeavor—at the very foundation of ethical behavior. In looking at propaganda, journalists will find many ideas about it, including manipulation, purposeful management, creation of desires, preconceived plan, reinforcement of biases, arousal of preexisting attitudes, predetermined ends, irrational appeal, specific objective, suggestion, and creation of dispositions.

From such terms as those just mentioned, one can gather a certain idea about propaganda. It seems that propaganda is related to an attempt by somebody to *manipulate* somebody else. By manipulate we mean *to control*—to control attitudes and actions. Propaganda, then, in a rather broad sense, is the effort or activity by which some communicator intends to manipulate the attitudes and actions of others by using techniques that appeal to ignorance, or emotions, or irrationality.

Although research has shown that the mass media have limited effects on opinion change, there are several effects that, although generally unintended, are sometimes deliberately used for manipulation. Thomas M. Garrett (1971, 57–58) refers to these effects as privatization, simplification, salience, and tempo.

Privatization causes audience members to withdraw into a private world when the mass media flood them with so much information that it is overwhelming and threatening. Or, such privatization can result from getting too many conflicting or contradictory reports. The audience members, in such cases, restrict their information consumption greatly and consequently deprive themselves of much important (albeit confusing) information.

Simplification is normally caused by time and space limitations, but journalists can intentionally restrict information in certain areas for a desired result. The journalistic manipulator knows that large segments of the mass audience do not really want to deal with complexity and intellectual refinement in a story. So the door is open for what might be called the propaganda of superficiality or stereotyping.

Salience (or the conferring of status) is an important manipulative device. Journalists can publicize or give salience to certain persons or issues by emphasizing them, by giving them attention repeatedly. This can also serve to distract audience members' attention away from other issues and persons. Often this is known as the agenda-setting function in journalism.

Garrett's last effect, the *tempo effect*, has to do with journalism's capacity to increase the pace of audience reaction. The almost instantaneous transmission of messages leads to superficial public understanding and to expectations that cannot be met quickly. This, in turn, often leads to unrest and frustration. When audience members do react, their responses are often inappropriate and emotional. This time factor can be used to manipulate audience members by journalists who desire to cause social unrest, or by those who wish to keep the public from carefully considering issues.

An additional problem is that propagandistic journalists may look at audiences as childlike. They assume that people generally can be treated as children who do not like to think, analyze, or question. Rather, according to such journalists, people like to be told, led, directed, helped, and guided. Aldous Huxley reminds us that simple messages, slogans, repetitive one-liners, marching songs, hymns, and singing commercials can be extremely effective propaganda messages because they appeal to the child in all of us. Huxley (1975, 278) writes that children "are highly susceptible to propaganda" because they are "ignorant of the world and its ways, and therefore completely unsuspecting." This proclivity, says Huxley, extends to many adults, whose "critical faculties are undeveloped."

The propagandist does not want the audience to analyze or to think seriously about the message. Nor is it expected that the audience will know the method or circumstances by which the journalist obtains the information, or the parts of the information left out, or the reasons certain aspects are played up and others played down or omitted. The propagandist does not want to be forced to deal in specifics or to present documentation or evidence. Harold Lasswell (1927) referred to the propagandist's orientation as *noneducational;* by this he meant that solutions have already been determined by the propagandist before the search for truth begins. Contrasted to this is the orientation Lasswell calls *nonpropagandistic,* which implies an unprejudiced and open search for the truth.

Pratkanis and Aronson (1992, 9) note that propaganda was originally defined as the dissemination of biased ideas and opinions, often through lies and deception. They point out, however, that as scholars began studying the topic more carefully, they realized that it is more complex, and that it has now come to mean "mass suggestion or influence through the manipulation of symbols and the psychology of the individual." This newer definition of propaganda makes it easier to include more and more journalism under the umbrella. It would now include the communication of a point of view, with the ultimate goal of having the receiver accept voluntarily a particular position.

Jacques Ellul and Eric Hoffer both have made the point that successful propaganda must be planted in fertile ground. In other words, propaganda must fill a need within a person in order for it to achieve its intended purpose. Ellul (1965, 41) writes that "a person listens to a particular propaganda because it reflects his deepest unconscious convictions without expressing them directly." Ellul illustrates this by noting that "because of the myth of progress, it is much easier to sell a man an

137

electric razor than a straight-edged one." Eric Hoffer (1951, 98–99) declares that propaganda by itself cannot invade unwilling minds, nor can it inculcate something completely new, nor can it keep people persuaded once they have ceased to believe. As Hoffer puts it, propaganda "penetrates only into minds already open, and rather than instill opinion it articulates and justifies opinions already present in the minds of its recipients. The gifted propagandist brings to a boil ideas and passions already simmering in the minds of his hearers. . . . He echoes their innermost feelings."

The PASID Formula

To help a person grasp the five essentials of propaganda, it might be well to look at the acronymic formula that Lowenstein and Merrill (1990, 244) refer to as PASID, which means that propaganda is *p*ersuasive, *a*ction oriented, *s*elfish, *i*ntentional, and *d*eceptive.

We can test a journalist's reporting against this formula. The journalist is a propagandist, we would maintain, if his or her story conforms to one or more of these five characteristics; the more characteristics that are present, the more obviously propagandistic the message.

1. *Persuasive.* Is the story intended to persuade? Does the journalist want audience members to believe something, to change an opinion, or to reinforce one? Persuasion is perhaps the basic or core ingredient of propaganda; one might say that propaganda is an attempt to persuade.
2. *Action oriented.* Does the story evidence a desire by the journalist to get somebody to take an action? With advertising, this is often quite obvious: The purpose is not just to persuade but to get the audience member to go out and buy something, or to take some action on the basis of the message. In mainstream journalism, however, it is often difficult to isolate this journalistic motive.

3. *Selfish.* Is there an egocentric motivation behind the message? Does the reporter want the reader to accept a particular viewpoint or set of facts that will be of some benefit to the journalist? Is there a selfish reason for the journalist writing a particular story or giving it a certain emphasis or slant?

4. *Intentional.* Is the message (which might be selfish, action oriented, and persuasive) created by the journalist in a predetermined or intentional way, so as to bring about the journalist's desired ends? Accidental persuasion, in other words, would not generally be considered propaganda.

5. *Deceptive.* Are various devices used by the journalist to deceive the audience member? Has the journalist been devious in the presentation of the story? Is there an attempt at honesty, fairness, balance, and objectivity in the story? The answer to such questions will go a long way in determining whether a story—or a journalist—is propagandistic.

In concluding this section on the PASID formula, let us look briefly at an example in journalism. Assume that a reporter is writing an election story. She has been assigned to cover the Republican candidate's speech in the state capital. It is a rather routine assignment. Ms. Williams, the reporter, is a liberal Democrat and she favors the Republican candidate's opponent (although, of course, she does not want this to be known by the readers of her newspaper). She goes to the capital, sits with the press, and awaits the speech. She wants to write a story that will reflect poorly on the Republican speaker (*intentional*); she wants to plant negative images in the minds of the readers, so that they will perhaps favor the opponent (*persuasive*) and ultimately vote for him (*action oriented*); she wants to do this because she prefers the Democrat and personally wants to be on the winning side (*selfish*). In order to achieve these ends, she chooses the most innocuous parts of the speech to play up, and she chooses the most illogical and ungrammatical quotes to use (*deceptive*).

Although all five characteristics of propaganda were used by this reporter, it is obvious that all would *not* have to be used in order for a story to contain propaganda. The final characteristic, deception, would actually be enough if it were done intentionally. Some students of propaganda would say that the action-oriented characteristic is not necessary for a message to be propagandistic, that the recipient being *persuaded* is enough and that the person has been propagandized even though no overt action is suggested. Other observers would say that some kind of action is implicit in *all* propaganda. For example, even if an advertiser doesn't *say* that the audience members should buy a product, the "seed is planted" and the intention is for a sale to take place.

Journalistic Propaganda

Many journalists maintain that propaganda is not only common in journalism but that it is vital and necessary as well. Echoing the words of French sociologist Jacques Ellul, such journalists believe that people actually desire propaganda, even need it, to reinforce their beliefs if not to change them. As Ellul (1965, 104) says: "Propaganda is . . . a means of *reinforcing* opinions, of transforming them into action. The reader himself offers his throat to the knife of the propaganda he chooses." Ellul believes that propaganda actually needs the mass media for its success, that journalists are prime propagandists, and that the middle and upper working classes of society are the most influenced by journalistic propaganda (106).

Since journalism is aimed largely at the masses, it is a perfect carrier of propaganda. Propaganda, Ellul says, has "an effect on the masses who lack any culture" (111). But, he points out, the most educated people (intellectuals) are also easily reached by propaganda. Therefore, journalists working for publications like *The New Yorker, The Nation, The New Republic,* or *National Review* can use propaganda with confidence that their educated readers will not completely be immune to it.

The propagandistic journalist adapts the propaganda to a

particular audience. Thus, when dealing with intellectuals, the propagandist simply adjusts the propaganda from a basically emotional to a more rational (or pseudo-rational) appeal. As Ellul notes:

> Naturally, the educated man does not *believe* in propaganda; he shrugs and is convinced that propaganda has no effect on him. This is, in fact, one of his greatest weaknesses, and propagandists are well aware that in order to reach someone, one must first convince him that propaganda is ineffectual and not very clever. Because he is convinced of his own superiority, the intellectual is much more vulnerable than anybody else to this maneuver, even though basically a high intelligence, a broad culture, a constant exercise of the critical faculties, and full and objective information are still the best weapons against propaganda (111).

At this point some readers may wonder if propaganda in journalism is necessarily unethical. What about "good" propaganda—that which attempts to get people to believe a certain way and take certain actions that will benefit society or help other people? This is the old "ends justifying the means" problem. Machiavelli might approve of it. Kant would not. Many ethicists have grave doubts about considering means as something really different from ends. As Kant put it in one version of his Categorical Imperative, we should treat people as ends only and never as means.

An ethical and morally concerned journalist certainly wants people to be helped and society to be better, but there are limits beyond which a journalist cannot and will not go. Philosopher Jay Newman (1989, 63–64) deals with this journalistic concern:

> A healthy-minded journalist seeks much more than the thrill of knowing that he has contributed to the reshaping of his readers' world views. He wants his readers to be better people for having read what he has written for

them. . . . he needs to be convinced of the objective
soundness or at least the overall reasonableness of the
particular ideas and attitudes that are being conveyed in
his reports and analyses.

Further, Newman emphasized that ethical journalists consistently avoid propagandizing. "When he [the journalist] habitually undervalues his own wisdom or habitually overvalues
that of his duller readers, he is on his way toward ending up as a
submissive panderer or . . . propagandist" (64). It would seem
that no journalists would want this to happen, but the very
nature of journalism exerts a magnetic pull toward propaganda,
and only the most ethical journalists can withstand it. Let us
now look at some of the ways in which journalists propagandize
in their journalism.

The Machiavellian Lure

The ideas of Niccolò Machiavelli (1469–1527), a Florentine historian and political philosopher, are attractive to many journalists
today (see box, p. 144). His well-known book *The Prince* (1513)
set the stage for the expedient, cunning, practical, and successful practitioner in social relations. American journalists, in seeking their objectives and in achieving their ends, often evidence
Machiavellian tendencies. Such tendencies, although they may
result in success, inevitably lead journalists away from ethics.

As I have pointed out (1992), Machiavellianism has a
strong appeal for today's journalists because it stresses a sense
of individualism, a desire for power, and an inclination to succeed. For the Machiavellian journalist, any action (or almost
any) is justified if it achieves the purposes or the ends desired.
This approach is in keeping with the hard-nosed, competitive
spirit of American journalism.

The key terms that dominate the philosophy of Machiavelli

include ambition, will, luck (*fortuna*), virtuosity (*virtù*), liberty, order, persuasion, ability, cunning, and courage. While most of these sound fine to the modern ear, the overall impact of Machiavellianism in the area of ethics is definitely negative. It is a philosophy that can be characterized as ends oriented, competitive, power based, egocentric, and pragmatic (success oriented). Machiavellianism does not comport with ethical concepts such as integrity, public betterment, honesty, sincerity, truthfulness, forthrightness, and altruism.

Are there Machiavellian journalists among us today? Most certainly. This is one reason journalism needs to give more attention to ethics. Advertisers and public relations practitioners are already sensitive to the implication that they are propagandists. They are, they say, simply in the business of persuasion and image creation; people know what they are doing and expect their kinds of messages. In other words, they embrace the success orientation of Machiavellianism, but they do so overtly. News-related journalists, on the other hand, are presumed to be presenting fact and truthful, unbiased stories; their professed loyalty is to objectivity. But many of them, like Robert Sherrill (1986), whom we discussed in Chapter 3, do adhere to propagandistic devices when they feel these are necessary to achieve their ends. The view of getting a story by any means is definitely a journalistic philosophy, but it is hoped that this is a minority position.

The ethical journalist should avoid such a philosophy like the plague because it is inauthentic and misleading. It has a certain appeal, to be sure, but it will lead the journalist into a quagmire of journalistic immorality wherein expediency and success take precedence over ethical considerations. Machiavellian journalism is the flip side of journalistic ethics—the dark underbelly of morality. The journalist who values personal authenticity, honesty, self-respect, public awareness, and social concern will repudiate Machiavellianism and will realize that there is something much more important than achieving one's ends.

Niccolò Machiavelli (1469–1527)

The brilliant Florentine historian and political advisor of the early Italian Renaissance, Niccolò Machiavelli, might well be called the "father of pragmatic, success-oriented journalism." Although personally a gentle and sensitive person, Machiavelli was a devotee of power and its cunning and courageous use.

Modern journalism's orientation toward success can certainly be traced back to the ideas Machiavelli stressed in *The Prince* (1514) and, to a lesser degree, in the *Discourses* (1519). He discussed the tactics of power and success that are reflected in many modern journalistic activities. Walter Lippmann has said that Machiavelli is one of the most reviled men in history, although he probably has the greatest following of them all.

Machiavellian journalism would be goal oriented, perhaps arrogant, and even abrasive. By all means, succeed, he would tell the modern journalists, and he would say to succeed by any means. He would want journalists to be virtuosos, relying on decisiveness and ingenuity. He would want journalists to be persistent and risk-takers, or as he said in *The Prince*, as strong as lions and as cunning as foxes. That, for Machiavelli, was *virtù*.

Seven Basic Techniques

We have been looking at propaganda in a broad, general way. Now let us turn to some of the specific devices or tactics that propagandists use. A starting place is to review the old, well-publicized list of seven propaganda devices described by the Institute for Propaganda Analysis in the 1930s. These devices

continued

Journalism, for Machiavelli, would be a self-defined, egocentric institution that leads and does not follow, except on rare occasions when it might be expedient to do so. The main mission of journalism, he would say, is to wield power and to influence society. Machiavellian journalism would be obsessed by its own freedom but would pretend great dedication to social responsibility. One aspect of freedom for the Machiavellian is to determine successful tactics. A newspaper or television station would be "responsible" when it got the story; that would be the ultimate journalistic end.

The Machiavellian journalist would not want to alienate people needlessly. Normal ethical rules should be used when they work but dumped when they are unsuccessful in reaching pragmatic journalistic goals. It would seem that Machiavelli taught *pragmatics*, not ethics, and such a philosophy closely resembles the hard-nosed stance of many modern journalists. Machiavelli's teachings are surely not for most journalists, but they are often followed, even if unintentionally.

are name-calling, testimonial, bandwagon, glittering generalities, plain folks, transfer, and card-stacking.

The *name-calling* device is used as a simple descriptor, with the journalist not wanting to provide evidence or details. Robert Doe, for example, will be identified as a *reactionary*, or *liberal*, or *draft-dodger*, or *patriot*, or some other negative or positive term. The journalist believes that the audience member will accept the description, vacuous though it is, simply because it is *said.* This is one of the oldest and most successful of the propaganda devices.

The *testimonial* device makes use of somebody's testimony about the worth (or unworthiness) of some political candidate, program, or product. When possible, the person quoted is someone with wide appeal, such as a sports figure, a university president, a governor, an outstanding musician, or a novelist. Here, the propagandistic journalist is substituting the *source* of a statement for real evidence of the quality of what is being pushed.

The *bandwagon* device appeals to people's desire to belong, to be part of the in-group. In short, the appeal is to a person's social instinct and the desire to be on the winning side. All kinds of journalistic linguistic techniques, such as predicting a win for someone, exaggerating crowd size, or even using or not using poll results, can exemplify the bandwagon device.

The *glittering generalities* device is often a favorite of the journalist. Here the journalist uses generalized and vague "virtue words" to get a desired reaction from the audience. Such terms as *progressive, courageous, virtuous, impressive, cooperative,* and *public-spirited* are designed to create an image that is not based on information or evidence.

The *plain folks* device is used by a journalist to make the audience members think of him or her as one of them. The propagandist is trying to show a commonality or understanding with the audience, being "just one of the folks." Like the bandwagon, it is an associational or identification technique and is often used by journalists, especially in columns and editorials.

The *transfer* device, perhaps used less often, is one that involves transferring to the journalist or the story the respect people have for some symbol, like the flag, the Bible, or the national anthem. If the journalist, for example, can quote prominent figures, heroes, and highly respected persons as

146

supporting a particular program or viewpoint, the propaganda value is enhanced. This is another associational device.

The *card-stacking* device is the most deceptive and certainly the most difficult to detect. The "cards are stacked against the truth" here, and only the dealer—the propagandist—knows the order of the cards. This is arguably the most dastardly of the devices because the journalist can lie, tell half-truths, exaggerate, eliminate stories or parts of stories, change or fabricate quotes and distort information in the stories. The card-stacking device is, without a doubt, the principal device of journalistic propaganda.

Other Propaganda Devices

What are some of the other commonly used journalistic propaganda devices? There are, of course, dozens of them, but the following are some of the most prominent.

Use of stereotypes Many journalists, in reporting and analyzing the news, regularly simplify the reality of people and events. They present persons and events as one-dimensional and static. They also tend to cast all members of a group as being more or less identical. This is the act of stereotyping, which provides a false (or at least an incomplete) image.

Selection of data Through the information selected to use in a story, the journalist can propagandize. What is selected and what is rejected is, of course, crucial to a story, so the propagandistic journalist can still be "accurate" while at the same time biasing the story through data selection. In this way, the journalist can concentrate on certain aspects of the story that fit into the desired "message" to be gotten across. It has been estimated that, in a typical daily newspaper, more than 75 percent of the potential news items of the day are not printed, and that the television viewer of the nightly news learns of only two or three of the hundreds of armed conflicts occurring throughout the world on that day (Pratkanis and Aronson, 1992, 224).

"I know something more" This device is very effective for journalists seeking to pry information from a source. But it is unethical, since journalists are telling a potential source that they have some information that needs to be responded to. The journalists insinuate that they have knowledge which they don't really have. Their intention is to get the source to comment on something for the record.

"Many people are saying . . . " Frequently, the reporter who is interviewing someone will lead into a question with a statement such as this: "Mr. X, many people are saying that your department has been secretive about your foreign travel during the past year. How would you respond to these people?" The way Mr. X *should* respond is by saying: "Who *are* some of these many people you mention as saying these things? Name one."

Unavailability for comment An unethical statement, which comes at the end of a story, goes something like this: "Mr. Doe was unavailable for comment." This type of statement usually is used in a controversial story in which something negative has been said about Mr. Doe. Such reporting imputes some kind of guilt to Mr. Doe, that he is hiding out or otherwise avoiding the press. It could be that the reporter called only once (didn't try hard enough to reach him), when Mr. Doe had stepped out of his office for a moment. But the reader of the story receives a different, and negative, message.

Tampering with quotations The reporter who wishes to create a certain image of a person, or to bias a story in a certain way, can change certain words in direct quotes or can quote out of context. A reporter can also fabricate quotes and attribute them to unnamed sources—a particularly unethical procedure. A kindred device is to use indirect quotes (or paraphrased versions of a statement) in which the reporter parlays a certain interpretation. In effect, this is similar to a poor translation of a message in a foreign language, but it is worse, especially if it is done intentionally.

Using opinion as fact A favorite technique is to present a journalist's opinion as if it were a fact. For example: "The audience gave the speaker an enthusiastic welcome." "Nobody doubted that Mr. X was criticizing the president out of desire for revenge." So much reporting of this type exists in journalism that a whole book could be written on this technique alone.

One person cross-section This journalistic device might also be called *inadequate or faulty sampling.* A reporter gets an opinion, for example, from a New York cab driver, about crime in the city; the story then quotes the cabbie in this way: "New Yorkers were incensed about the rise of crime in the city. David X, of the Bronx, said that he is thinking about moving out of the state if something is not done soon to correct the problem." Are New Yorkers incensed? How many of them? Most of them? A few of them? The reader simply does not know. One person's opinion has been projected onto the entire population.

Biased attribution How a journalist attributes information to a source can indicate propaganda—can create a certain image of a person. For example, an attribution verb such as *said* is neutral (it is not opinionated and evokes no emotional reaction). On the other hand, such attribution verbs as *snapped, hissed, shouted,* and *sputtered* reflect negatively on the speaker. Such verbs as *remarked, responded, smiled,* and *explained* create a positive image of the speaker. Adverbs accompanying such verbs can further reinforce the negative or positive impact of the image.

Misleading headlines Headline writers can propagandize effectively because they know that, by and large, people come away from stories with the substance of the headline—not the story—in their minds. In addition, there are many readers who see the headline but never read the story. Headlines can easily be twisted, biased, distorted, and otherwise rigged so that they bear about as much resemblance to the stories as the stories often do to the events they purport to mirror.

Biased photographs The news photographer can present heroes from the best perspectives—smiling, positive, calm, and dignified. Enemies can be photographed from the worst perspectives—frowning, nervous, impatient, and ridiculous. Photographs may not lie, but they can convey misleading images. Like facts and quotations in a news story, photographs can be selected for a particular purpose. Anyone who carefully observes photographs in newspapers and magazines, and pictures on film or television, can see the practical tactics of photographic propaganda.

Repetition If you scrutinize a newspaper that you know has a particular bias, you will note that certain themes, persons, ideas, and slogans appear week after week. A reader of a "liberal" daily like the *Washington Post* can get caught up in the newspaper's repetitive pattern of news presentation, editorial stand, and so forth. This reader can predict exactly what "line" the paper will take on almost any event or issue. The regular reader of the *Wall Street Journal* can do the same thing. The same repetitive themes also can be discerned on television. As politicians and advertisers know very well, repetition is among the very best propaganda devices.

Appeal to authority This technique is closely related to the testimonial device discussed earlier. It relies heavily on support from well-known and reputable sources and authorities. The journalist may attribute a statement to a veiled authority or quote selectively from a prominent person's statement. Or, a journalist might quote a suspicious or discredited source, depending on the effect desired. In some news stories, there are "leading educators" or "prominent theologians" who are saying something; there may be some Pentagon spokesperson giving out information, or some "source close to the president" who is taking a particular line. If a commentator wants to make a certain point for the television audience on a controversial subject, it might be wiser to quote some prominent person (who has a similar position) than to give the opinion directly. This might be called the device of "hiding behind some compatible authority."

Stressing the "enemy" A potent tactic of propaganda in journalism, in both news and interpretation, is emphasizing the negative—of being *against* something or somebody, spotlighting the "enemy." Journalists appear to find it much more exciting, for example, to be against government leaders than to be *for* them. They seem to relish the idea of criticizing established institutions, thereby often lending support to social forces that are violent, irrational, atypical, and destructive. This technique might also be called the "antiestablishment" device, or perhaps the more common "watchdog function."

Using fiction Journalists may, on occasion, camouflage fiction and present it as fact. This is a common technique in many third world countries, but varieties of it can be found in the United States and other developed countries. Journalists do not totally fictionalize, but they may mix some fiction (or conjecture) into the fabric of a fact-based story. They may not have everything needed to make a good, complete, compelling story, so they do a little "creative" fictionalizing. Gaps may be filled in with certain made-up quotations that *sound* as if they are real. After all, nobody will ever know, except perhaps the source, and what recourse will he or she have? The source probably won't even remember if a certain thing was said or not.

News management The journalist may not like this term, preferring news decision making or something less negative. But the journalist does, indeed, manage the news in the sense of omitting certain stories or parts of stories. The journalist calls this practice "writing or editing news," not censorship or management. A British authority on propaganda, J. A. C. Brown (1963, 16) says that such propaganda takes two forms: (1) "the selective control of information to favour a particular viewpoint," and (2) "the deliberate doctoring of information in order to create an impression different from that originally intended."

Selective factuality Here the journalist uses specific and exact information and quotations in regard to some persons and "sanitized" or doctored material from others, depending on the intent to provide a positive or negative image. An example: "The president snapped, 'I ain't going to put up with this crap any longer' " *as opposed to* "The president reassured the Congress that he was determined not to continue condoning the practice."

Letters to the editor Through printing or not printing certain letters from readers, the journalist can effectively propagandize. This device gives the journalist an obvious advantage over the letter writer; the journalist can ignore the letter, can print all of it or some of it, or can insert a retort at the end of the letter, thus having the last word.

A Final Word

In this chapter we have discussed the broad dimensions of propaganda, attempted to define it, focused on its danger to journalistic ethics, and pointed out many of the propaganda techniques used in journalism. Few would doubt that some (perhaps even many) journalists participate in propaganda, either by originating it or by conveying the propaganda of others. At any rate, it is safe to say that modern journalism is saturated with propaganda in its many forms. It is clear that as propaganda increases in journalism, ethics is in retreat.

It seems appropriate, in conclusion, to quote these words of Jacques Ellul (1965, 257), the eminent French writer on propaganda:

> It is merely convenient to realize that the side of freedom and truth for man has not yet lost, but that it may

well lose—and that in this game, propaganda is undoubtedly the most formidable power, acting in only one direction (toward the destruction of truth and freedom), no matter what the good intentions or the good will may be of those who manipulate it.

ANALYZING ETHICAL ISSUES

1. Do you think it is fair to consider advertising as propaganda? Does the PASID formula, when applied to advertising, lend credence to its being propagandistic? What is the primary objective of the advertiser? Of the public relations person? If these persons are propagandists, how are they different from propagandistic journalists?

2. As you watch a network news program, can you discern any propaganda? Specify the kinds you find. How could the news director have eliminated such propaganda? How do television news programs build up stereotypes? Can you give an example of a *national* stereotype perpetuated by television of some country or its people? What network anchor do you think is the most propagandistic? Why?

3. When a newsmagazine (for instance, *U.S. News & World Report*) selects an overabundance of "conservative" sources to quote, or when National Public Radio uses mainly "liberal" stories, does this exemplify propaganda? Why or why not? Does the question just asked in itself indicate propaganda? Explain your answer.

4. If a news photographer were to come on your campus to do a series of pictures to accompany a story, and if he were negatively biased for some reason against your school, what are some of the ways he could give a bad impression through his photographs? How could you take the same *types* of pictures that he took but give a positive impression of the school? Do you think it is easier or harder to propagandize through pictures than through words? Why?

5. Is one implying a certain kind of propaganda when one says, for example, that the *Washington Post* is a liberal newspaper and the *Wall Street Journal* is a conservative newspaper? How does a newspaper show or indicate its ideological bias except through propaganda? Name and comment on a few ways that would, or would not, be propagandistic.

References

Brown, J. A. C. *Techniques of Persuasion: From Propaganda to Brainwashing.* Baltimore: Penguin Books, 1963.

Ellul, Jacques. *Propaganda: The Formation of Men's Attitudes.* New York: Alfred A. Knopf, 1965.

Garrett, Thomas M. "Manipulation and Mass Media." In *The Manipulated Man,* edited by Franz Bockle. New York: Herder and Herder, 1971.

Hoffer, Eric. *The True Believer.* New York: Harper & Row (Perennial Library), 1951.

Huxley, Aldous. "The Arts of Selling." In *Ethics and the Press: Readings in Mass Media Morality,* edited by John C. Merrill and R. Barney. New York: Hastings House, 1975.

Lasswell, Harold. "The Theory of Political Propaganda." *American Political Science Review,* vol. 21 (1927).

Lowenstein, Ralph, and John C. Merrill. *Macromedia: Mission, Message and Morality.* White Plains, NY: Longman, 1990.

Merrill, John C. "Machiavellian Journalism." *Journal of Mass Media Ethics,* vol. 7, no. 2 (1992).

Newman, Jay. *The Journalist in Plato's Cave.* Teaneck, NJ: Fairleigh Dickinson University Press, 1989.

Postman, Neil. *Amusing Ourselves to Death.* New York: Penguin Books, 1986.

Pratkanis, Anthony R., and Elliot Aronson. *Age of Propaganda: The Everyday Use and Abuse of Persuasion.* New York: W. H. Freeman, 1992.

Sherrill, Robert. "News Ethics: Press & Jerks." *Grand Street 5,* no. 2 (winter 1986).

Stoler, Peter. *The War against the Press: Politics, Pressure and Intimidation in the 80s.* New York: Dodd, Mead, 1986.

CHAPTER SEVEN

KORZYBSKI TO
THE RESCUE

Journalists work in the field of language; words are the basic tools of their craft. Along with other communicative symbols, such as pictures, words construct the "maps" to the territory of reality. Since language affects thought, and thought affects action, it is easy to see how the meanings we attach to words relate to the field of journalistic ethics. The orientation called general semantics, *expounded by the Polish philosopher, Alfred Korzybski, provides seminal concepts related to words, their meanings, and their implications. An orientation to general semantics will raise the linguistic consciousness of journalists, bring them to a higher level of sophistication, instill in them a recognition of the weaknesses and the power of words, and generally help them overcome the enslaving tendencies of language. In this chapter we will look at some of the basics of general semantics, including the need for a multivalued orientation; the recognition that language always leaves out part of reality, the idea that language fails to keep up with constant change; and the inadequacy of labels to express essence.*

As we saw in the last chapter, propaganda largely uses language to ensnare the unsuspecting listener or reader. Since words are powerful tools in the hands of the communicator, the ethically concerned journalist will want to use the language clearly and accurately, so as not to fall into the seductive trap of semantic manipulation.

One of the ways both communicators and audience members can become sensitive to the dangers of propagandistic language usage is to consider the orientation called *Korzybskian* or *general semantics.* In this chapter, we shall try to show how an awareness of semantics can help minimize propaganda and help journalists to be more ethical.

Why is a study of semantics helpful? Journalism ethics has to do with the responsible and knowledgeable use of language. We need, therefore, to look at how the words used by journalists affect thinking and how thinking affects actions. This is the thrust of general semantics, a theory of language formulated by Alfred Korzybski (1879–1950).

Korzybski's book, *Science and Sanity: An Introduction to Non-Aristotelian Systems and General Semantics* (1933), is not easy to read. We are fortunate, however, that there have been reliable "translators" of Korzybski, people such as S. I. Hayakawa, Stuart Chase, Wendell Johnson, Charlotte Read, Kenneth Johnson, J. S. Bois, Irving Lee, and Harry Weinberg. These and other writers have brought the thought of Korzybski to the general reader and have tried to make applications to many areas of our society.

The ethical journalist wants to use language as precisely and as effectively as possible in order to present people, events, situations, and ideas in a realistic and helpful manner. As any journalist knows, to do so is not easy. Korzybskian semantics may well provide a useful model for precise and vivid journalism. It can aid the journalist in understanding the limitations of language, the tremendous power of language, and the ways language affects one's thinking and action. It will also provide clues as to how to avoid propaganda in journalism.

A general semantics orientation (see Figure 7-1) will also help a journalist to be careful in using language, to respect its potency, to understand its weaknesses, and to take a more

FIGURE 7-1
GENERAL SEMANTICS

Similar Perspective:
Buddhism

Influences:
Heraclitus
B. Russell
L. Wittgenstein
A. Einstein
H. Poincaré
A. L. Whitehead

Followers: ◄——— **Alfred Korzybski**
S. I. Hayakawa   *Science & Sanity* (1933)
Charlotte Read
Stuart Chase
Wendell Johnson
Irving Lee   **SIX MAIN PRINCIPLES**
J. S. Bois   *"Flux"*
Kenneth Johnson Avoid denying change.
Earl English   (static language/dynamic reality)

"Map Is Not Territory"
Avoid confusing label with reality.
(word/label is not the thing)

"ETC." (principle of "non-allness")
Avoid assuming you have said all about anything.
There is always more that can be added.

"IS" of Identity
Avoid verbal simplification.
(John Doe is a lawyer. He is much more than that.)

Individualization
Avoid stereotyping.
(Arab-1 is not Arab-2; Ph.D.-1 is not Ph.D.-2)

Stay Low on Abstraction Ladder
Avoid highly abstract words.
("cow" better than "animal"; "Bossy" better than
"cow"; actual cow out in reality better than any
label)

scientific approach to language. Many readers may say that Korzybskian principles are no more than common sense, but as Korzybski was fond of saying, common sense is really not very common.

Korzybski and General Semantics

How does language affect human behavior? This is the basis of a study of general semantics. General semantics is not, as journalism educator Donald Ranly (1984, 138) has said, a study of the meaning of words; rather, he says, "it studies how words come to be what they are and how they came to mean what they mean to various people at various times." Ranly points out that general semantics is not concerned with the *correct* meaning of words. Instead, general semantics shows that words have *many* meanings, or that the meanings are in the minds of people, not in dictionaries.

Korzybski's Eclecticism

Korzybski (see Figure 7-1) was interested in what he called the "time-binding" capacity of human beings—the ability to inherit the accumulated achievements of previous generations, to develop them, and to pass them on to subsequent generations. Thus, human beings have a unique dimension. Korzybski, in considering the consequences of such time-binding, recognized that the main way such a process can take place is through language and other symbolic forms.

Korzybski was extremely eclectic in his interests and knowledge and was particularly influenced by the work of Bertrand Russell, Alfred North Whitehead, Henri Poincare, Ludwig Wittgenstein, and Albert Einstein. He tried to relate the implications of their work to his new area of general semantics, and he believed that all of our basic linguistic doctrines and our basic education needed to be revised to match the new more scientific outlooks (Read, 1975, 244). We have no reason to believe that Korzybski was influenced by Friedrich Nietzsche, but many of their views of language and reality are very similar (Pula, 1992). Nietzsche's ideas were around and it is likely that the well-read Korzybski was influenced by them. It is possible, however, that the insights were arrived at independently by both men. Here is a brief excerpt from a 1873 essay by Nietzsche showing clear affinities with the general semantics perspective on language and truth:

> If somebody hides a thing behind a bush, seeks it again and finds it in the selfsame place, then there is not much to boast of, respecting this seeking and finding; thus, however, matters stand with the seeking and finding of "truth" within the realm of reason. If I make the definition of the mammal and then declare after inspecting a camel, "Behold a mammal," then no doubt a truth is brought to light thereby, but it is of very limited value, I mean it is anthropomorphic through and through, and does not contain one single point which is "true-in-itself," real, and universally valid, apart from man (1992, 65).

That a person creates meaning—or truth—is a fundamental general semantics principle, as reflected in Nietzsche's words. Other foundational pillars of Korzybski are that the world and all in it are dynamic and constantly changing; that reality is holistic, not segmented and separate; and that concepts are multivalued, not two-valued. Korzybski wanted us to use language in a more scientific manner, trying always to make our words approximate reality better. He wanted us to be more precise while at the same time being more flexible and less static in our language. Certainly this is an important orientation for the journalist.

Korzybski believed that the old Western way of thinking

and using language, which he attributed primarily to Aristotle and which he bemoaned as unscientific, should be superseded by a more realistic and dynamic language. Thus, he developed his system, which he and his disciples referred to as *non-Aristotelian*.

Ranly (1984, 138–39) has emphasized that journalists should assume the Korzybskian mode and write and speak as scientists. He says that scientists are adaptable, they test everything, they are discriminating, they know that things change, and they are willing to change their minds. He believes that journalists should have this same scientific attitude. Another scientific stance for the journalist would be to take a rather aloof demeanor—standing back, observing calmly, questioning insistently, and recording carefully. As Ranly and others have pointed out, just as general semanticists urge a scientific approach, so also should journalists.

General Semantics and Buddhism

Other cultures have also emphasized what are basically general semantics principles. This has been especially true in the Orient. In an earlier work (1981), I summarized the many ways that the ideas of Korzybski are similar to those of Buddhism, especially Zen. There is no direct reference to Buddhism in Korzybski's basic work, and not much is known about his intellectual influences, but Buddhist ideas either made an impression on him or this eclectic Polish thinker generated similar ideas independently.

Another writer on general semantics, J. Samuel Bois (1961, 46), also has noted the similarity of Buddhism to the Korzybskian orientation, especially as the two relate to basic purpose: "General semantics is an attempt to pierce the walls of our own culture. From our Western ranks an advanced party of mathematicians and physicists have made their way through these walls. There are social scientists who keep busy widening the breach, so that the common people may pour out of the confining fortress and establish their homes in the lush valleys of non-aristotelian systems. A conscientious study of Zen belongs to this program of liberation."

Here is a short list that shows at a glance how Korzybskian semantics and Buddhism share a close relationship (Merrill, 1981, 35–45):

1. Both recognize the validity of a nonsymbolic communion with the "real" world—the "silent level" of Korzybski and the "nonmental observation" of Zen.
2. Both insist that nature is all of a piece, divided only by language.
3. Both accept a kind of Whorfian hypothesis that expresses a theory of linguistic relativity in which a people's thinking and behavior are determined by the character of their language.
4. Both are suspicious of symbols, especially verbal ones. As Korzybski puts it: "Whatever you say a thing is, it is not."
5. Both accept impermanence and reject permanence; for example, dog-A is never identical with itself.
6. Both reject universality, stressing that differences are more basic than similarities, that uniqueness should be emphasized more often.
7. Both reject the substance view of reality and emphasize the process of becoming, of change, of flux.
8. Both stress the impotence of language, the value of silence, and the unspeakable or silent levels of reality.
9. Both accept the merger theory of reality, where everything is all of a piece, divided only by language.
10. Both believe that language distorts reality and that one must try to achieve a kind of deverbalization, a kind of oneness with *real* or nonconceptual reality.
11. Both view all existence as momentary, made up of ever changing particulars in various clusters, all in constant flux, arising and ceasing.
12. Both draw a distinction between the world of concepts and words and the real world—reality itself.

Korzybski's Basic Principles

Let us now summarize some of the core principles of general semantics. Certainly this is not an exhaustive list. These principles are the ones that appear to have the most significance for journalists, although it is safe to say that all of Korzybski's philosophy would be of interest, if not of practical utility, to those working in journalism. It should be noted that general semantics relates significantly to the aspects of ethics dealing with objectivity and truth, which we discussed in Chapter 5.

The word is not the thing As general semanticists say, "The map is not the territory." The symbol is not the object or event that is symbolized. As Stuart Chase (1938, 8) has put it, "We are continually confusing the label with the nonverbal object, and so giving a spurious validity to the word." The thing that is called *dog,* he points out, is a nonverbal object; it can be described, observed by the senses, and then conveniently labeled *dog.* But the label is not the animal. This principle is even more important when we get to abstract labels like *freedom, justice, patriotism, professionalism,* and *responsibility.* Even the common labels *journalism* and *news* cause all kinds of semantic problems.

Stay low on the abstraction ladder Keep high abstractions to a minimum, the general semanticist would say. Don't use abstract terms when you can use more meaningful—more specific—ones. Instead of *dog,* one could use *collie;* or instead of *collie,* one could use the specific collie's name, *Mac.* But *dog* is certainly preferable to *animal* and much preferable to something like *entity.*

Making clear distinctions: reports, inferences, and judgments Reports are scientific, based on observable data, and verifiable. *A report:* John Doe, age thirty-nine, was sentenced yesterday to ten years in prison. Inferences are assumptions made from known data. *An inference:* John Doe will soon be in prison. Judgments are conclusions made from inferences. *A judgment:* John Doe is an evil and dangerous person. Journalists often confuse or mix these three, and faulty inferences or faulty judgments can have a negative impact on ethical behavior. The preceding comment is an inference itself, modified somewhat by "*often* confuse" and "*can* have a negative impact." The journalist must be careful.

Recognition of non-allness General semanticists also call this the "etc. concept," which means it is impossible to say everything about anything. There is always something left out of a report, thus the idea of "et cetera" being tacked on to any verbal report or description. A report may say "He is a Chicago lawyer." So he is, but he is much more (a father of three, a husband, a Methodist, an ex-football player, a Marine veteran, and so on). Journalists, in using language, must omit much significant information. The issue for ethical journalists is that they should not intentionally bias their story by what is left out, and they should be conscious of the omissions.

Static language, dynamic reality Reality is constantly changing, but language largely stays the same. The University of Missouri today is not what it was in 1940 or in 1993, although it retains the same name. Bill Clinton is not the same Bill Clinton today that he was yesterday, although he may still be in the White House (which itself is a constantly changing house).

General semanticists get this principle of constant flux from the pre-Socratic Greek philosopher Heraclitus, who said something like "No person steps in the same river twice." The river has changed. It is in essence a different river the second time the person steps in it and, indeed, the person who steps in is not the same person.

We should mention Nietzsche again here, for he believed, like Heraclitus, that existence is constantly in flux. He even went so far as to deny *being* since everything is always *becoming* (Shutte, 1984, 40–41). He believed that using nouns to refer to what is becoming misleads the user of language, that the stability of things is not to be inferred from the formal

163

structure of language. Like Korzybski, Nietzsche viewed language as imposing a stabilizing fiction on reality, on a world that is constantly coming into being and passing away.

This view of a dynamic reality, contrasted to the static nature of language, is indeed an important concept for the journalist. In a sense, if we take this notion too far, the conclusion would be that nothing is ever anything and therefore that journalism cannot deal with such a world of ever changing essences. We know, however, that journalists must try to do just that; they must at least draw "good maps," as Korzybski might put it.

These concepts of dynamic reality expressed by Nietzsche and Korzybski are quite similar to those espoused by the famous Chinese philosopher, Chuang Tzu, who lived at about the same time as Heraclitus (ca. 250 B.C.). This greatest of all the Taoist writers whose historical existence can be verified expressed several general semantics concepts, especially that all beings are in a state of flux. As Thomas Merton (1965, 15–17) has pointed out, Chuang Tzu, like Heraclitus, believed that what is good and pleasant today may, tomorrow, become evil, and what is impossible today may suddenly become possible tomorrow. Like Heraclitus and the later general semanticists, Chuang Tzu put little faith in words and formulas about reality but concentrated, instead, on the direct existential grasp of reality itself.

Swede-A is not Swede-B Members of the same group, or those carrying the same label, are discrete individuals; they are not the same, and it is dangerous to make assumptions about them because of their nationality, race, religion, party, or other characteristics. This is an antistereotyping principle.

Multivalued orientation This is a very important general semantics principle. It is contrasted to a two-valued, either-or orientation, which Korzybski associated with Aristotle. According to the general semanticists, it is unrealistic to categorize people as either good or bad, tall or short, conservative or liberal, ugly or beautiful, thin or fat, stupid or intelligent, slow or fast, altruistic or egoistic, and so forth. People, and other entities in the world, are more complex and are normally combinations of many attributes. The problem of the two-valued orientation can be highlighted by asking a question such as this: How tall does a short person have to be before that person becomes tall? At the root of this problem, say the general semanticists, is that language (English at least) is basically composed of words that are opposites. Thus, the language itself *forces* us to think in opposites and to build up our biases to conform with them. What we need to do, Korzybski would say, is to indulge in a kind of spectrum thinking wherein tall merges with short, liberalism with conservatism, and so forth, all along a scale or spectrum. Thus, we would think of country-A's press as neither authoritarian nor libertarian, but a mixture.

Beyond the "is" of identity According to the general semanticists, reporters overuse the "is of identity." This means that we oversimplify reality with our verb *is*. This concept is similar to one we mentioned earlier, that the word is not the thing, or the map is not the territory. The symbol *New York* is, we say, a large city. But actually, *New York* is a label and not a city at all. We are aware of this when we stop to think of it, but as Stuart Chase (1938, 8) says, "the trouble is that we do not stop to think about it." The "is of identity" is illustrated by Chase when he notes "the child's remark that 'Pigs are rightly named, since they are such dirty animals' " (9).

General semantics through the years has addressed a broad array of subjects dealing with language (including cultural relativism, euphemisms, metaphor, objectivity, and doublespeak), but as Murphy (1992, 126–27) emphasizes "through it all the verb *to be* has remained a core of concern." Murphy quotes George Santayana as writing, as far back as 1923, that the "little word *is* has its tragedies" because it "names and identifies different things with the greatest innocence; and yet no two are ever identical, and if therein lies the charm of wedding them and calling them one, therein, too, lies the danger." According to Murphy, Santayana was referring to locutions like "Peter is a man" and "Peter is cold," in which the *is* implies "the coupling of equivalent things, whereas in fact in the first case it joins nouns that have different levels of abstraction and the second case joins a noun to an adjective that neither completely nor permanently describes it" (127).

Subjectivity of descriptive adjectives Reporters often think they are reporting or giving factual information when, in fact, they are simply expressing their own opinions. Most adjectives probably tell more about the person using them than about what they purport to describe. Journalists may use such descriptors as "an enthusiastic audience," "a beautiful painting," "impressive architecture," and the like. With these descriptions, nothing really is being said about the audience, the painting, or the architecture; there is only some clue, perhaps, to the reporter's concepts of enthusiasm, beauty, and impressiveness. Such language in journalism is self-reflexive; it is useful only in that we can learn something about the evaluative criteria of the reporter.

Natural tendency to bias Journalists must recognize a tendency to select (or abstract) from reality those portions that are consistent with personal values. What is chosen for a story may be what is appealing, what coincides with preferences, and what gives pleasure. Reporters trying to be fair and objective need to be always on guard against this egoistic proclivity. Ethical or fair journalists must force themselves to include information that is unpleasant to them and with which they disagree.

Journalists, General Semantics, and Ethics

Now that we have surveyed the main tenets of Korzybski's general semantics, let us focus on what it might mean in journalism. More specifically, we need to see how general semantics has a special significance for journalists concerned with ethics.

In journalism, as we have seen, ethics is closely related to the use of language: in journalists' reports, evaluations, critiques, analyses, and other forms of written and spoken discourse with mass and specialized audiences. Ethical journalists use language ethically, considering the truthfulness, the precision, the impact, and the long-term consequences of the words used. Unethical journalists, on the other hand, are careless with language. They do not recognize the power of words; they do not consider carefully the consequences of certain messages; they do not understand the intricacies and complexity of language; and they do not seem to care about the harm and misrepresentation that can come from a nonscientific linguistic orientation.

Journalists who want to be ethical must make an effort to use language skillfully and with a minimum of distortion. In order to do this, according to the general semanticists, they must first of all discover their biases. It is easy for journalists to present biased stories. Yet caution needs to be exercised here because the bias may be with the readers of the news story and not with the writer. As S. I. Hayakawa says (1939, 42), when a newspaper carries a story we don't like, omitting facts we think important and playing up certain facts in ways we consider unfair, we are tempted to condemn the paper for unfairly slanting the story. But, he points out, we assume that what seems important or unimportant to us would seem equally important or unimportant to the journalists. We are making an inference about the writer of the story or about the editors. The assumption of bias leads us to believe that the editors deliberately made the story misleading. Such an inference, according to Hayakawa, is not rational; it may well be that our (the readers') bias is the problem.

Nevertheless, a story may have been deliberately slanted by the journalist. Avoiding bias or slanting is certainly in keeping with ethics, with being impartial and fair. As Hayakawa points out, it is "more importantly a matter of making good maps of the territory of experience" (43). The biased reporter cannot make good maps; too much will be left out, and the map will tend to be one-dimensional and misleading. The journalist who is ethical and who writes well will look at the same subject from many perspectives and will, therefore, draw for the reader a good map, one that is reliable.

General semantics would insist that the concept of "etc." be applied to the thinking of the journalist. While recognizing that not everything can be said in a story, the sophisticated and ethical journalist will *always try* to put as much information in the story as possible. Certainly no information will be left out because of personal bias.

Of the main principles of general semantics already summarized, probably one of the most important for journalists is the avoidance of highly abstract terms. Journalists trying to be ethical should avoid terms that paint a highly favorable or prejudicial picture of a journalistic hero or villain. Stuart Chase (1938, 21) suggests that we look at verbal passages carefully, trying to identify abstract words and phrases that don't have discoverable referents—and substituting a *blab* for every meaningless term. He calls the *blab* a "semantic blank" where nothing really comes through. Journalists, then, using a high degree of "blab" language, communicate very little.

One may take any newspaper and scrutinize a story for blab language. Take this hypothetical sentence, for example: "The American society today, steeped as it is in multicultural sham, has retreated into a dark abyss where every kind of verbal description is tinged with implied prejudice and other demeaning implications." Translated into blab, it would read: The blab blab today, blabbed as it is in blab blab, has retreated into a blab blab where every kind of blab blab is tinged with blab blab and blab blab.

The ethical journalist with a general semantics orientation will avoid the either-or or two-valued verbal perspective, or what is called the Aristotelian orientation. Wendell Johnson (1946, 7–8) explains this well. Johnson notes that Aristotle said, in short, that people talk and act as if a thing is what it is—that A is A. This is the *law of identity.* Aristotle also assumed that anything must either be some thing or it is not that thing, that anything is either A or non-A. This is called the *law of the excluded middle,* which general semanticists call the two-valued way of thinking. According to Johnson, Aristotle believed that people take for granted that something cannot be some thing and also not be that thing. In other words, something cannot be both A and non-A, which is called the *law of noncontradiction.*

Laws of logic such as these formulated by Aristotle often mislead us, according to the general semanticists. The logic suggests that something that is good must be all good (identity); that which is not good must be bad (exclusion); and that nothing can be good and bad at the same time (noncontradiction). General semanticists (Hayakawa, 1939, 222), however, believe that good and bad are usually mixed and that it is often impossible to impose such "simplistic categories upon experience." As Hayakawa says: "The difficulty with Aristotle's 'laws of logic' is that while they *seem* to be sensible, in fact they are inadequate to deal with reality, forcing us to press it into narrow confines."

Perceptive journalists know that the either-or perspective is not realistic. For example, people are not so simple as to be either conservatives or liberals. Each person is liberal in some areas and conservative in others. Liberals, for instance, may be conservative in the sense of wanting to conserve their particular values, and some persons are social liberals but economic conservatives. Ethical journalists recognize this complexity in language and will try to tell about people's specific beliefs and values rather than using labels, which only tend to separate people into opposite camps.

Hayakawa stresses that Korzybski was interested in a multivalued or infinite-valued logic (not a two-valued Aristotelian one). He goes on to say that because Korzybski called

169

general semantics a "non-Aristotelian system" it is claimed that he was fighting Aristotle. This is not the case, says Hayakawa (1939, 222). Korzybski "was simply fighting insanity, whether individual or national." As for Aristotle, Hayakawa concludes that "he must have been one of the sanest men of his time; but anyone whose knowledge and thinking are limited to Aristotle's can hardly behave sanely in *our* time."

Recognizing that group labels are unfair for describing individuals is a general semantics principle that is closely tied to journalistic ethics. Iranian-A is not Iranian-B; overweight-A is not overweight-B; communist-A is not communist-B; doctor-A is not doctor-B; African American-A is not African American-B, and so forth. Journalists, if they are to be ethical, should hammer this principle into their very souls. It will help them eliminate stereotypes, will lead to individualizing persons in stories, and will thereby help journalists make better maps of the real territory out there.

Eliminating, or at least explaining, abstract words in a story is necessary for the ethical journalist. When terms like *pornography, patriotic citizens, good Christians, arrogant government officials, fundamentalists,* or *concerned voters* are used in a story, it is incumbent upon the journalist to explain them. If possible, the journalist should give specific examples of what these subjects do or what they believe, in order to shed some light on the terms.

The concept of flux or change is one of the most important general semantics principles for the serious, responsible journalist. It is tempting for the journalist to assume that people are always what they have been, that they don't change or have different opinions, that they remain entrenched in a static way behind their static names. It is also tempting to believe that institutions, political parties, cities, rivers, highways, and so forth never change—that New York today is the same New York as it was yesterday, that Senator-A believes the same thing this week that he believed when someone interviewed him last month, that Harvard University today is the Harvard of 1980. Things change constantly, and the ethical journalist will recognize and incorporate such changes in every story. For example, the ethical reporter will not use an old quotation (as if it were currently valid) giving someone's views on a subject, even if that quotation were obtained the day before yesterday.

General semantics will help the journalist recognize that human perception is not a simple stimulus-response act, nor is it ever complete. Russell and Many (1993, 294) say that such a recognition "may begin to demonstrate what has been called maturity and good news judgment." An event, for example, is out there in reality; it is what it is in all of its completeness and trueness. Reporter-A comes to the event and perceives it, or portions of it, and this perception is different from that of reporter-B. What this means is that there always will be differences in reports of the "same" news events. But, say Russell and Many, "If they [reporting students and reporters] can be taught their observations are by definition incomplete, perhaps they will learn to ask even more questions and search for more sources and vantage points before concluding they have observed and reported everything" (294–95).

As we have seen, the Korzybskian perspective can be extremely helpful to those journalists who want to make better maps of the territory and who want to be as flexible as possible with the static language available to them. People and places constantly change, but their names remain the same. This is an inherent difficulty in journalism, a problem that is actually insurmountable. Only sensitive journalists will succeed in this area of ethics.

One of the main difficulties, say the general semanticists, is that most people hardly ever think about such Korzybskian emphases. Therefore, they fall into poor language habits that provide only a one-dimensional, inflexible world in which concepts are drawn in either-or terms and people and institutions are depicted as static, stereotyped entities. Most journalistic maps are poorly drawn; the lines are fuzzy and significant details are left out. A new sensitivity to language, coupled with a recognition of its potent impact on thinking and action, will enable journalists to be more ethical, to become more symbolically sophisticated, and to draw progressively more reliable maps of the complex and rugged territory of reality.

ANALYZING ETHICAL ISSUES

1. What are some of the ways reporters could use the general semantics principle of flux (for example, John Doe-1992 is not John Doe-1996, or the U.S. Congress-1988 is not the U.S. Congress-1995)? If reporters take the principle *too* seriously (carry it to an extreme), how would it affect their reporting? How can reporters indicate that everything is *becoming*, that nobody or no thing *is?* Is there really a need to do this in journalism? Explain.

2. Do you think journalists use abstract words (such as *patriotic*) too casually? Should they specify what they mean by such words as *conservative, left-winger, freedom fighter, progressive,* and *nationalist?* How could a reporter allude to, or describe, a person (such as Rush Limbaugh, or Jesse Jackson, or Mother Theresa) without using abstract terms or labels?

3. Do you think that a multivalued orientation (avoiding either-or thinking) is a good and useful concept for the journalist to adopt? Why or why not? What are you—a liberal or a conservative? What are you—a subjectivist or an objectivist? What are you—a good student or a bad student? How does this general semantics principle (of avoiding a two-valued orientation) relate to the problem of stereotyping in journalism?

4. What are some of the ways reporters can guard against biasing their stories? Or should they? Are there any journalists without biases? What does bias mean to you? Are you biased against it? If bias is a normal or natural thing, why should we try to avoid it?

Korzybski to the Rescue

5. Get a story from a local newspaper and bring it to class. Underline
   all of the words in the story that are semantically difficult—those
   that may not be understood by all readers in the same way. Do
   your class members have a common understanding of these
   words? Can you rewrite the story, eliminating these problem
   terms? How do you do it?

References

Bois, J. Samuel. "General Semantics and Zen." *ETC.*, vol. 18 (1961).
Chase, Stuart. *The Tyranny of Words.* New York: Harcourt, Brace, 1938.
Hayakawa, S. I. *Language in Thought and Action.* New York: Harcourt, Brace, 1933.
Johnson, Wendell. *People in Quandaries: The Semantics of Personal Adjustment.* New York: Harper & Row, 1946.
Korzybski, Alfred. *Science and Sanity: An Introduction to Non-Aristotelian Systems and General Semantics.* Lakeland, Conn.: International Non-Aristotelian Library Publishing Co., 1933.
Merrill, John C. "Korzybskian Semantics and Buddhism: Some Philosophical Parallels." In *Building Bridges across Cultures*, edited by Nobleza C. Asuncion-Lande and Emy Pascasio. Manila: Solidaridad Publishing House, 1981.
Merton, Thomas. *The Way of Chuang Tzu.* New York: New Directions, 1965.
Murphy, Cullen. "'To be' in Their Bonnets, A Matter of Semantics." *ETC.*, vol. 49, no. 2 (summer 1992).
Nietzsche, Friedrich. "Truth and Falsity in an Extra-Moral Sense." Portion reprinted in *ETC.*, vol. 49, no. 1 (spring 1992).
Pula, Robert P. "The Nietzsche-Korzybski-Sapir-Whorf Hypothesis." *ETC.*, vol. 59, no. 1 (spring 1992).
Ranly, Donald. "Words and What They Do to People." In *The Writing Book*, edited by George Kennedy et al. New York: Prentice-Hall, 1984.
Read, Charlotte S. "General Semantics." *ETC.*, vol. 32, no. 3 (fall 1975).
Russell, Charles G., and Paul Many. "Using General Semantics Principles in the Basic News Reporting Classroom." *ETC.*, vol. 50, no. 3 (fall 1993).
Schutte, Ofelia. *Beyond Nihilism: Nietzsche without Masks.* Chicago: University of Chicago Press, 1984.

CHAPTER EIGHT

THE TUFF FORMULA: TRUTH OR CONSEQUENCES?

Every reporter wrestles with this question: How firmly must I dedicate myself to the truth? Other questions follow from that one: How thorough must I try to be in my story? Is leaving verified and relevant material out of my story being untruthful? How is being biased or unbiased related to the truth? What should my position be when my concept of fairness tends to conflict with my concept of the truth?

Such questions get us into the very heart of journalistic ethics. In this chapter, the TUFF formula for ethical reporting is presented. It brings into focus the very questions just posed, plus others. For example, can—or should—reporters try to be truthful, unbiased, full, and fair in the report? Such basic and complex questions are considered at some length in this chapter.

As we enter the area of ethics more specifically related to the reporter, we encounter situations in which being truthful often conflicts with other goals, where various types of deceit raise their tempting heads, and where a belief in the public's right (or need) to know collides with other considerations. In this chapter, we will deal with the complexities reporters face as they try to be truthful, unbiased, thorough, and fair.

174

The TUFF Formula: Truth or Consequences?

I developed a formula (Lowenstein and Merrill, 1990) that challenges both the skill and ethics of the reporter. It is called the TUFF formula, and it highlights the characteristics usually considered essential for a good report or a good reporter; it can be looked at as both a professional and an ethical formulation. It is difficult ("tough") to adhere to this formula, but it does provide a worthy ideal for the conscientious reporter. There are some interesting, and perhaps unresolvable, problems with the TUFF guide, and these will be discussed later. First, let us look at the basic concepts of the TUFF formula.

TUFF Formula: Basic Meaning

The formula provides four concepts (see Figure 8-1) that will guide reporters in turning out reports that are professionally done and ethical. Good and ethical reports are truthful, unbiased, full, and fair. Let us look at each of these characteristics.

The "T": Reports Should Be Truthful

We have already dealt at considerable length with truth and its cousin, objectivity (in Chapter 5), and we have noted the problems connected with truthful reporting. The fact remains, however, that seeking the truth (and presenting it if and when possible) is a fundamental professional and ethical tenet of journalism. The good reporter is expected to be dedicated to providing the truth; this is a kind of professional imperative, at least in American journalism. When it comes to ethics, the picture is somewhat different and problems arise, but we shall discuss these later. At present, it is enough to say that the first letter in the TUFF formula is perhaps the most important of the reportorial guidelines.

It is easy to say that a journalist should be truthful, but what exactly does that mean? Revealing everything the reporter

FIGURE 8-1
NEWS REPORTER'S ETHICS: TUFF

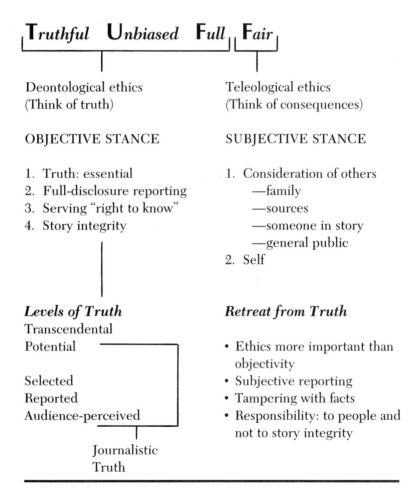

Truthful **U**nbiased **F**ull **F**air

Deontological ethics
(Think of truth)

Teleological ethics
(Think of consequences)

OBJECTIVE STANCE

SUBJECTIVE STANCE

1. Truth: essential
2. Full-disclosure reporting
3. Serving "right to know"
4. Story integrity

1. Consideration of others
   —family
   —sources
   —someone in story
   —general public
2. Self

Levels of Truth
Transcendental
Potential

Selected
Reported
Audience-perceived

Journalistic
Truth

Retreat from Truth

• Ethics more important than
  objectivity
• Subjective reporting
• Tampering with facts
• Responsibility: to people and
  not to story integrity

176

knows about a story? Telling what is considered the main part of the truth but not the whole truth? Simply being accurate in reporting the facts? Providing some truthful perspectives but missing others? Questions of this type can go on and on, because the very nature of reporting always seems to limit truth in some way. Reporting, after all, is a process of *selection* from reality. We must remember that reportorial truth is always partial and incomplete. What any story contains is but the tip of the proverbial iceberg sticking above the waters of perception.

The "U": Reports Should Be Unbiased

Just what is in an unbiased story? Who is the unbiased reporter? The realistic (or cynical?) answer to such questions would be that *no* story or reporter is actually unbiased. Bias is built into one's subjectivity and manifests itself throughout the total process of journalism.

When we refer to being unbiased in reporting, we are really talking about having an *attitude* toward being unbiased—a persistent desire to provide an unbiased report. We will never be totally free of bias, of course, because all reporters have values and their own ways of selecting and structuring information. Good reporters, though, can refrain from putting *intentional* bias into their stories.

The First "F": Reports Should Be Full

The concept of fullness or thoroughness suffers from the same intrinsic problems as the preceding one. No report can ever be really complete. Something will always be left out, for the reporter's selective capabilities and perceptions necessarily lead to only a partial report. As the general semanticists say in their principles of non-allness, nobody can say everything about anything. Fullness is an ideal, a goal for reporters to strive for, even though they cannot reach it. In fact, all of these

177

concepts in the formula are *destinations* toward which reporters travel. Good reporters certainly try to get as much pertinent information into their stories as possible. Although all
stories may be incomplete to some degree, good reports are
more complete than the mediocre or poor ones.

The Final "F": Reports Should Be Fair

This last concept in the formula is perhaps the most troublesome, because it takes reporters from a more objective level
of concern to a more subjective one. It also takes them out of
the pure land of professional reporting and squarely into the
realm of ethics. Reporters should want to be fair, and the attitude of fairness is a very important characteristic.

The Paradox of Reporting

Reporting is the most demanding and the most traumatic enterprise in journalism. It is certainly the most troublesome in that
there is the relationship between the concept of full-disclosure
reporting and the concept of journalistic teleology, with its emphasis on a consideration of possible consequences. Reporters
with a professional hard-nosed approach concentrate on, or
emphasize, *the report* and the correspondence of the facts to
the actual event being reported. Their primary loyalty is to the
truth, the first concept of the TUFF formula. As the general
semanticists would say, the truth-oriented reporter wants to
make the best possible map, while realizing that the map "is
not the territory."

"Truth-Oriented" Reporters

These reporters (whom we will call truth-oriented) have a
basic loyalty to the story itself, to its integrity, to its being
unbiased and complete. They might be called *pure* reporters;

they consider it their duty only to provide a truthful account, to put out the facts (which are verifiable) in a meaningful context, and to let the chips fall where they will. In other words, they report; they do not worry about consequences. These reporters might be called Kantian journalists because they feel duty bound to follow the *a priori* rule of truth-telling and are not concerned with the possible results.

These reporters are convinced that letting their biases and values affect the story—distorting, changing, adding, or subtracting—damages the basic integrity of the report. In other words, truth-oriented reporters recognize that the duty of a reporter is to present the facts of the case; to provide as much of the truth as possible; and to try to make the story conform, as closely as possible, to reality.

"Think-of-Consequences" Reporters

A second type of reporter, while paying lip service to the truth, is willing to deviate from the truth when possible or likely consequences demand it. These are the *teleological* reporters, those who believe that it is irrational to stick to some rule or maxim absolutely, as the deontologists do. The morality of the act is what they prize. These think-of-consequences reporters are the anti-Kantians, the relativists, the reporters who see deviating from the truth on occasion as the *ethical* thing to do. Since these reporters are concerned about consequences, they are naturally dedicated to *the acts* that will bring about their desired consequences.

Their view of morality is also connected to acts. They subscribe to what is called the direct view of ethics (Hudson, 1986, 2–7), in which the question is What ought I do in this particular case as I consider my act's ramifications? The question is not What should I do as a natural consequence of my basic nature and character? (the Aristotelian indirect view), but rather What action that I take will make me ethical in this case? In other words, the act-connected direct view gives primacy to the moral evaluation of acts, and considers the general moral character of the individual as secondary.

Usually, these reporters have gone from the "TUF" of the formula to the final "F," where they are trying to be fair and are putting greater emphasis on predicting possible consequences than on full-disclosure reporting. In a sense, these reporters are being less than reporters for ethics' sake. They are often tempted to deviate from basic reportorial principles because of some possible consequences that might accrue if full-disclosure reporting were done. The motivation for such deviation might be egoistic or it might be altruistic: It really doesn't matter, for the damage to the integrity of the report occurs when the reporter steps out of the strict reportorial mode and into the moralistic or fairness mode and tampers with the facts.

Let us look at a common example. A reporter who knows the rape victim's name but chooses to leave it out of the story has slipped from the reportorial mode into the fairness mode. All kinds of *reasons* can be used to justify such an action— possible embarrassment to the victim or her family, or even possible further danger to her—but these are subjective, opinion-based justifications having to do with possible consequences, not with a full-disclosure report. Should a reporter use in the story the name of a fourteen-year-old girl who has been beaten, raped, and sodomized? It would be difficult, we think, even for the truth-oriented reporter to reveal that name, although some full-disclosure reporters might think they should.

Here is another case. What about a story on the existence of an undercover police operation that might destroy the investigation and even endanger the life of an undercover agent? Again, it would be easy to justify withholding this story because of the possible consequences. Revealing or excluding information based on a consideration of consequences can no doubt be justified in an ethical sense. But journalists who do so might well wonder about their dedication as *reporters*. Such journalists also should not be too hasty to condemn government officials who may indulge in exactly the same type of behavior and for similar reasons.

Resolving the Quandary

We can see, then, that the TUFF formula, while perhaps useful in a general way, is somewhat troublesome. The gap is wide between the first three letters and that final fourth one. Some reporters are dedicated only to the first three; others consider the fourth one the key part of the formula.

Is there any way to resolve this quandary: the reporter's dedication either to truth or to consequences? Perhaps there is. The full-disclosure reporter, the one dedicated to truth and not to consequences, could be considered the ethical one because of this dedication. This, of course, simply applies the ethical theory of Immanuel Kant to the truth-oriented reporter. If these truth-oriented reporters do a good job of writing a story, if they get as close to reality as possible, they have done the responsible, ethical thing.

Such reporters would be ethical so long as they did not tamper with the truth, and so long as they reported forthrightly and fully disclosed the relevant and verified facts. When they deviated from this deontological ethical approach—when they omitted the name of a rape victim, for instance—they would be deviating from their professional role as reporters. Therefore, we can say that these truth-oriented reporters are as ethical as the consequentialists; they simply march to a different ethical drummer—in this case, Immanuel Kant. Said another way, they represent Aristotle's indirect view of ethics: They believe that being ethical means having a basic *character* of honesty

181

and forthrightness, whereby the virtue of their journalistic acts rests on the moral nature of the person who does such acts and not on the specific acts themselves (Hudson, 1986).

There is another possible resolution to the truth versus consequences quandary. That is to envision a reporter as having one foot in each camp—in the truth-oriented camp and in the consequentialist camp. Thus, we could take the position that this is not an either-or ethical choice. Reporters might say that they are dedicated to the truth *generally,* but that from time to time, as the situation calls for it, they are willing to tamper with the truth for sound, ethical reasons. One problem with this approach is that such reporters do not have a clear-cut ethical theory, but rather one that shifts back and forth between principle and consequences. It is therefore difficult for journalists to know when they are ethical or unethical. It is indeed difficult to serve two masters.

Further Thoughts on Fairness

Since we are dealing with ethical journalism, perhaps more attention should be given to the fourth characteristic in the TUFF formula, fairness. We would assume that every journalist wants to be fair. But the problem arises immediately: Fair to whom? Or to what? In trying to answer such questions, the intrinsic subjectivity of fairness comes to the fore. Quite often, when reporters are trying to be fair to one person, they are unfair (at least in somebody's eyes) to another. Perhaps fairness, like beauty, is in the eye of the beholder.

Paul Johnson's Commandments

The British historian and media critic, Paul Johnson (1993, 20), has given as one of his "ten commandments" for the media that *media must have a general fair-mindedness.*

The TUFF Formula: Truth or Consequences?

Johnson states: "If ever there were a moral quality, it is the ability to be habitually fair because it involves so many others: the imagination to see other points of view, tolerance of them, temperance, and restraint in expressing your own, generosity and, above all, a rooted sense of justice." He also points out that "fair-minded newspapers stick out a mile—because they are so rare."

Johnson suggests five other commandments that relate to being fair-minded: a willingness to admit error, a respect for words, an overriding desire to discover and tell the truth, a consideration of consequences, and an urge to educate. But being fair means different things to different people, and the concept of "fair reporting" is fraught with semantic difficulties. Perhaps we can profitably analyze some of the meanings of this term. Let us begin with Johnson's elements of fair reporting.

A willingness to admit error We know that many journalists (and mass media) are very sensitive and defensive. They are quick and eager to point out the errors of others but are often reluctant to shine a light (or have one shone) on their own failures and errors. One aspect of being fair is to admit and, when possible, to correct errors. Media that refuse to admit and correct errors evidence arrogance.

Law journal editor Steven Brill (1989, 10) refers to the libel suit brought by Israeli general Ariel Sharon against *Time* magazine. When the magazine responded to a request to admit a mistake, it said "that it didn't make corrections on its own but would deign to print letters from others to correct the record if its editors thought the record merited correction." According to Brill, Sharon basically was told "to get lost"—that the magazine "stood by" what was later revealed as a false and concocted story.

A respect for words If journalists were as sensitive to words as they are to criticism, their stories would be much fairer than they are. Words are powerful, and the careless or improper use of them can be extremely unfair (as the preced-

183

ing words may be to journalists) both to the substance of the story and to the various parties involved in the story. Reporters must learn to choose words carefully so as to project the exact meaning and image that is intended. This is not easy, as good reporters know, but it is essential for reporters who want to be fair.

A desire to discover and tell the truth It should be clear that if a reporter is not concerned with the truth, it will be extremely difficult to conceive of fairness. The hard work in journalism comes when a reporter refuses to accept glib explanations, first impressions, or surface events, but goes on to obtain by all ethical means possible, the actual core of the story. Then, once the truth is uncovered, the reporter must have the courage to tell it.

A consideration of consequences When we normally think of fairness, we think of possible consequences, and consequentialist ethics is a perfectly legitimate stance. What is likely to happen that will be harmful to this or that person if we publish this story or this bit of information? Such questions show a concern for fairness. It is impossible, really, to consider fairness without thinking to some degree about consequences. We can see, however, that this commandment can conflict with the preceding one, telling the truth. If we consider the consequences of telling the truth and decide that they are bad or harmful, we must then make the difficult decision to conceal or reveal.

An eagerness to educate If we want to be fair to someone, we are normally concerned about giving that person useful and accurate information in a meaningful context. In short, we want to educate. We want to provide valid, not erroneous, views of various aspects of reality. This desire to educate should surely mirror the complexity of the story. Christians, Rotzell, and Fackler (1987, 105) state that "as a minimum," fairness involves coverage that "reflects the degree of complexity inherent in the events themselves." It is very difficult to report fairly on complex issues, and for this reason the job of the reporter is the most difficult in journalism.

SPJ *Code:* Another View of Fairness

Having dealt briefly with some of Johnson's commandments related to fairness, let us turn to some other characteristics that might also help to define this difficult term.

Protecting confidential sources The Society of Professional Journalists' *Code of Ethics* (1987) and others propose that such protection falls within the purview of fairness. If the reporter promises not to reveal a source's name, for example, and then proceeds to do so, it is evident that fairness has somehow been damaged. In this sense, fairness is related to keeping promises, to being dependable.

Respecting the dignity and well-being of people This characteristic, along with the next four, are found under Section 5 of the SPJ *Code.* The message comes through loudly: respect others—their dignity and well-being. Just how the reporter might do this is not spelled out, but it is related to being fair to others. Maybe fairness would require the reporter to get the message across to the audience.

The Associated Press Managing Editors organization, in its proposed new ethical code, has dealt with three aspects of fairness (Shepard, 1994, 40). Here are the statements:

> 1. Opportunity to reply: In reporting any statements that could injure the reputation of an individual or group, those affected must be given the earliest opportunity to reply.
> 2. Courtesy and compassion: Special care should be taken to treat sensitively those who are unaccustomed to dealing with the press.
> 3. Developments: When stories have been prominently displayed, fairness requires that substantial subsequent developments be covered and similarly displayed.

185

Surely the concept of fairness goes beyond these three areas, and in one sense, it permeates the whole body of ethical discourse. We can at least say that journalistic fairness hinges on the idea of human dignity and on respecting that dignity. Thus, reporters should exercise care in using clichés, prejudices, and insensitive language. Christians, Rotzell, and Fackler (1987, 105) mention that the *New York Times* "warped its news account" about an Indian battle back in 1890 by using biased labels such as 'hostiles' and 'reds,' 'bucks' and 'squaws.' " The *Times* might argue that there is a need to read words in the context of the historical period in which they are used, but readers cannot be expected to be so discerning.

Giving the accused a chance to reply Fairness would dictate that someone accused of something in a story should have the opportunity to respond.

Guarding against invading a person's privacy This would seem to be part of a basic respect for others. Although privacy is a very complex concept, the journalist who wants to be fair will take care not to intrude into the lives of private individuals. Special care should be taken not to invade the privacy of persons in times of anxiety, tragedy, and sorrow.

Quoting people accurately and in context Fairness demands that what one is reported to have said is actually what that person did say. It would be unfair for the journalist to take someone's words out of context, to twist them and distort them, so as to give a flawed report of the statement.

Correcting errors promptly and completely It is obviously unfair to let errors persist in the public mind. When errors are made, the journalist should correct them as quickly and thoroughly as possible, or to the full extent that the particular mass medium's policy will allow. If, for example, the policy says that corrections cannot be made, then the onus falls on the policymakers and not on the journalist who might want to make corrections.

The TUFF Formula: Truth or Consequences?

The Problem with the Final "F"

As we have seen, the final "F" (fair) in the TUFF formula can have a large number of meanings. Many characteristics may be combined to comprise what we mean by fairness. One way of putting it would be to say that the term has many *connotations* and really no *denotation*. It is interesting that a popular thesaurus (Morehead, 1978) gives these synonyms for *fair: impartial, equitable, just,* and *moderate.* Actually, these synonyms are as semantically fuzzy as *fair.* However, it might be helpful to look at them briefly and extract what meaning we can from them.

The reporter should be impartial This means that there should be no bias in the report, that the reporter has put aside personal biases and prejudices in an attempt to be fair. Not to favor any one side in a controversy is the core of impartiality. It requires that the reporter have a kind of dispassionate, neutral stance in reporting. This, of course, is very difficult to achieve, since a reporter *must* distinguish among persons, facts, quotations, and perspectives, deciding that some are more valuable or important than others. A reporter necessarily passes judgment on the ingredients of a story, and it is hard to do this with impartiality.

One aspect of impartiality that we should mention involves taking care not to treat one person one way and another person another way in the basic news coverage. Even in photographs, impartiality is important, as Joann Byrd of the *Washington Post* discovered in 1993. Kate McKenna (1993, 43) tells of Byrd writing a column (in response to readers' complaints) on whether the newspaper had deliberately used mostly flattering photos of Bill Clinton and less than complimentary shots of Ross Perot and George Bush. The column concluded that there was a good reason for the readers' complaints. The *Post* had not been impartial, and therefore not fair, in its picture coverage.

The reporter should be equitable A story that is fairly reported should show some kind of equity or evenhandedness in emphases. It should give a proper balance. Does *equitable* mean equality in the sense of pure balance (as in television time or newspaper space)? Some journalists might respond to such a question in this way: Being equitable in a story means my giving the kind of representation to aspects of the story that I think most accurately reflects the reality of what I am reporting. If this is the general journalistic concept of equality, then it is little more than personal determination and slides into the chasm of relativism.

The reporter should be just The semantic problem appears here as well. What does "being just" mean for a reporter? What is justice in journalism? Who can define the term? One reporter may think it is just to report on the details of a crime; another may believe it to be unjust. One reporter may think that reporting the crudities of a president or quoting exactly his ungrammatical remarks during an interview is just. Another might believe that justice is served by omitting the crudities and paraphrasing the remarks so as to hide the poor grammar. Perhaps we can say that being a just reporter is exactly what is meant by being a fair reporter—giving "proper" consideration (another subjective concept) to all parts of a story.

Henry Hazlitt (1972, 335) makes the point that justice must be judged by its results, and that "whatever produces bad results, whatever reduces material welfare or human happiness, cannot be justice." Hazlitt goes on to define justice (fairness) as "the system of rules and arrangements that increase human peace, cooperation, production, and happiness, and injustice whatever rules and arrangements stand in the way of these consequences."

The reporter should be moderate This last synonym is about as vague as the others. If reporters are to be fair, presumably they will be moderate. If this means pulling one's punches (for example, not calling a thief a thief or a rapist a rapist) then it would seem to fly in the face of fairness, or at least in the face of honest and truthful reporting. Surely a reporter would want to be moderate in the sense of not being extreme, if the latter meant exaggerating the substance so much that it did not substantially match reality. If moderate means precise and accurate, then certainly the reporter should be moderate.

In conclusion, although the TUFF formula may be of general help to the reporter trying to be ethical, it has some built-in problems, mainly stemming from the final "F." The first three letters of the acronym—truthful, unbiased, and full—are more objective and more compatible with rule-oriented or deontological ethical theory. The final letter, however, slides over into a more subjective mode, where teleology (concern for consequences) becomes the prime ethical motivation. We return again to the early question: Is the reporter mainly concerned with truth or with consequences?

Perhaps the answer most often heard is that the reporter is concerned with *both*. This, of course, sounds good, but when ethical crises arise, a reporter must face the basic dilemma of taking a stand for truth or being willing to deviate from it. In either case, as we have pointed out, the reporter is being ethical in the sense of conforming to an ethical theory. Whether the emphasis is put on *truth* or on *consequences,* the reporter should have good reasons for all positions or actions taken. But every reporter will always have to face the basic quandary inherent in the process of reporting—the paradox of the first "T" and the final "F."

ANALYZING ETHICAL ISSUES

1. Is it possible for someone to be both a full-disclosure reporter (unbiased, thorough, and truthful) and a fair reporter (someone who considers ramifications to the principals of a story and other consequences)? How does the TUFF formula relate to the basic loyalties of the reporter? How is being unbiased as a reporter

different from being truthful? From being full (or thorough)? How would you define *reporter*? How would this differ from your definition of a *journalist*?

2. In regard to fairness, the SPJ *Code of Ethics* says the journalist should respect the "dignity and well-being of people." Which people are being referred to? What is meant by the "well-being of people?" What about *dignity*? How would a reporter follow this guideline in covering a criminal story, such as a story about rape or a murder trial? Is it fair for a reporter to refer to aboriginal Americans as *Indians*? African Americans as *blacks*? Homosexuals as *gays*? Rebellious fighters as *terrorists* or *freedom fighters*?

3. If a reporter mainly takes the direct view of ethics (assessing *acts*) and she does a journalistic act that pleases her (such as hiding the name of a juvenile offender), would she be more a teleologist or more a deontologist? Would she be ethical? Another reporter takes the indirect view (looking not at the act but at herself and her basic character). Would this journalist be ethical or unethical regardless of how she wrote the story?

4. Do you think a reporter should be dedicated to the truth? Why or why not? Doesn't this conflict with the concept of journalistic freedom? If you think truth is absolute and universal, explain how a reporter can obtain it. If you think truth is relative and contextual, does this mean that a dedication to truth is only to *somebody's version* of truth? How does an audience member cope with this? Discuss the *New York Times'* longtime motto: "All the news that's fit to print." Give your views on this definition of the news: News is whatever someone wants to call news.

5. How do you think the biblical Golden Rule applies to the basic job of the reporter? Should the reporter report the story of a murderer—his crime, arrest, trial, and so forth—in the same way that he would like to be treated *if he were on trial for murder*? If the reporter applied this test, do you feel it would affect the way he wrote his stories? In what ways? Is Golden Rule ethics egoistic or altruistic? Is it based on the teleological or on the deontological theory of ethics? Do you think a good reporter

The TUFF Formula: Truth or Consequences?

should accept Golden Rule ethics or rise above its subjectivity to a more objective stance? Explain your position.

References

Brill, Steven. "Admitting Mistakes Is Anathema to Most Journalists, but They Are Wrong." *TJFR Business Journalism Review* (fall 1989).

Christians, Clifford, Kim Rotzell, and Mark Fackler. *Media Ethics,* 2nd ed. White Plains, NY: Longman, 1987.

Hazlitt, Henry. *The Foundations of Morality.* Los Angeles: Nash Publishing, 1972.

Hudson, Stephen D. *Human Character and Morality.* Boston: Routledge & Kegan Paul, 1986.

Johnson, Paul. "The Seven Deadly Sins of Journalism." *The Spectator* (London), 16 January 1993.

Lowenstein, Ralph, and John C. Merrill. *Macromedia.* White Plains, NY: Longman, 1990.

McKenna, Kate. "The Loneliest Job in the Newsroom." *American Journalism Review* (March 1993).

Morehead, Philip D., preparer. *Roget's College Thesaurus.* New York: Signet Books, 1978.

Shepard, Alicia C. "Legislating Ethics." *American Journalism Review* (January–February 1994).

Society of Professional Journalists. *Code of Ethics.* 1987.

CHAPTER NINE

ISSUE ANALYSIS: SOURCES AND QUOTES

In this chapter we discuss a common ethical problem: dealing with news sources. Deceit in some form can carry over into many aspects of the journalist's relationship with sources: the way in which quotations are handled, the manner of actually attributing statements, and the failure to identify the person being quoted. All kinds of questions arise regarding the reporter's relationship with sources. Which quotes from the source will be used? When the journalist promises anonymity to the source, should such a promise always be kept? What would be the exception, if any? What about the responsibility to the audience—the so-called people's right to know? How friendly should the reporter be with the source? These and other pertinent questions are dealt with in this chapter, which provides a look at a more practical area of moral reasoning.

As we approach the end of what has been primarily a theoretical journey through journalism ethics, we perhaps should stop to consider some of the ramifications of a more practical and common ethical problem. Although many ethical problems could be chosen, we will look at the issue of news sources and apply moral reasoning to specific journalistic cases.

Every act of news gathering, editing, and writing or speaking the story impinges on morality; ethical decisions must be made all along the way. Therefore, when we talk about a television journalist's general demeanor, gestures, shrugs of the shoulders, or facial expressions, we are talking about things that can be related to ethics. Who are the people giving us information? Which of their words do we use and with what emphasis? How do we go about attributing their words to them?

One of the most troublesome areas in journalism ethics involves dealing with news sources. We are referring especially, to *human* news sources, not to records, diaries, transcripts, and so forth, although these are important and sometimes troublesome as well. This chapter will concentrate on *people* who are news sources, on the way they are quoted in stories, and on the way statements are attributed to them. These are three sides of a reportorial triangle, each of which poses ethical pitfalls to the conscientious and competitive journalist.

In any consideration of journalistic sources and their remarks, basic questions present themselves immediately: What kinds of sources are needed for this story? Who will be one of these sources? Why this source instead of another? Are there any personal or ulterior motives for having such a source? Which statements from the source will be used? Why these statements and not others? How will the statements be framed—directly or indirectly, in context or out of context? What reportorial methods will be used to attribute the statements to the source?

Such questions get us into the ethical quicksands that are found in this aspect of journalism. The answers to such questions give us a clue as to how serious a journalist is about ethics.

A Look at the Sources of Stories

It is obvious that certain kinds of stories require certain kinds of sources. A reporter writing a piece about a nuclear reactor and its possible danger to a community is not going to interview a local musician. A story about education will most likely have as its main sources various teachers or school administrators. This is not always as it should be, but it is what usually occurs. It makes sense. Once the *kind* of source is determined, the problem becomes more complicated. Then the question is *which* particular source (among the educators, for example) will be used and probably quoted?

Sometimes a source will be chosen for rather frivolous (or provocative) reasons. For example, early in 1995, CBS television's Connie Chung put a microphone before Speaker of the House Newt Gingrich's mother, and as the cameras rolled, Chung asked her what her son thought of the president's wife, Hillary Clinton. Chung told Mrs. Gingrich that what she said would just "be between you and me." Chung was told that Newt considered Mrs. Clinton "a bitch," and the story went worldwide. Chung had fished for a provocative story, had gotten it, had betrayed a promise, and had put another black mark beside the ethical performance of the news media.

Choosing the Sources

There are several criteria for making decisions about which sources to use. First, a source is needed who is knowledgeable in the area of the story and who has credibility. Most journalists also like to pick sources who are articulate and interesting and who can express themselves clearly and perhaps even in memorable "sound bites." The problem, quite often, is that the most knowledgeable person may not be the most articulate. This poses an ethical problem for the journalist.

There are other decisions to be made as well. The reporter needs somebody right now, so as to get the story ready for the 6 p.m. newscast or the late edition of the paper, deadlines that are coming up within an hour and a half. Who is available? What source can be found in time? This is often what determines the source that is actually used. Let us assume, however, that one good (credible, articulate, and knowledgeable) source is secured. Is that enough? Will this source adequately *represent* the dominant thinking among experts on the subject? Generally not.

Even a good source would likely create bias in the story, which goes against the second letter of the TUFF formula, that the story should be *unbiased*. The reporter probably believes that the source is a good representative, but this opinion is quite subjective, and the good reporter will want to diminish this subjectivity as much as possible. Bias is a constant threat, and the reporter can never really *know* the representiveness of a source without considerable and sophisticated research.

There is another problem with using only one source. It will make the story one-dimensional and may make some audience members suspicious that the source has been intentionally selected to provide a certain bias or position. The reporter might need several sources. The reporter needs to consider the third letter of the TUFF formula: fullness or thoroughness. Now the reporter will search for other sources to provide several statements about the particular issue. He or she will want to find sources with different perspectives. No reporter wants to include only harmonious sources; disagreement and contention always make a better and more complete story.

Through all of this, the ethical reporter will exercise great care so as not to get sources who will simply say what the reporter thinks about the situation. Too often, sources are selected who actually "speak for" or reflect the personal biases of the reporter. Many journalists use this technique, making sure to quote their sources accurately so that they can say the story was accurate and objective. In some cases, this is no more than a reporter's own propaganda put in the mouth of a compatible source. The ethical reporter should try diligently not to fall into this practice.

Using Anonymous Sources

A highly controversial issue and one fraught with much ethical significance is whether or not to name your source. There is no unanimous agreement among journalists on this question. Some, but not most, newspapers have strict rules against the use of anonymous sources; others permit it in certain cases, and still others simply leave the decision up to the reporter.

The American Society of Newspaper Editors (ASNE), in its Statement of Principles, says that "unless there is clear and pressing need to maintain confidences, sources of information should be identified" (Cranberg, 1990, 26). That's clear enough, but there seems to be one small problem. What exactly is "clear and pressing need to maintain confidences"? This opens the door to subjectivity and variances among journalists, all subscribing to ASNE's principles.

The Society of Professional Journalists (SPJ), in its *Code of Ethics* (1987), does not give us much help on the issue. The *Code* says that "so-called news communications from private sources should not be published or broadcast without substantiation of their claims to news values." This is a real mouthful and raises a number of questions rather than giving any meaningful answers.

What, for instance, does the *Code* mean by "so-called news communications"? And why mention only those from "private sources"? We are told that such communications should not be used by the journalist "without substantiation of their claims to news values." What does that mean? If I am a journalist, am I simply to *substantiate* their "claims" to news values? How do I do it? Do I ask the originator of the "so-called news communications" if he or she will say that these messages have "news values"? Presumably, yes. Thus, I substantiate "their claims" by hearing their claims. Once the claims are substantiated, I can publish or broadcast them. But as an ethical journalist, I am still unsure about using material from these private sources, and I also wonder about material coming from public sources.

Let us get back to secret—or anonymous—sources. Many journalists maintain that much information cannot be obtained without some sources being kept secret. So the journalists promise confidentiality and say it is only ethical that they keep their word to the sources. This is well and good, but a prior question needs to be asked: Should reporters promise confidentiality in the first place? After all, one important characteristic of a report is that it is verifiable, that it is truthful. For example, perhaps I see in the newspaper that some "university source" has said that the Missouri School of Journalism is going to be phased out next year. How can I verify the statement? Or, how can I even find out who is putting out such a rumor? The TUFF formula warns against such tampering with the truth—in its very first letter. With anonymous sources, audience members are at a distinct disadvantage, not knowing *who* said such and such and thereby not having a chance to ascertain its validity.

Anonymous sources mainly impinge on ethics when they are quoted as saying something negative, derogatory, or false about someone. The person tainted by the source's words has no recourse. Even an accused person on trial has the right to face the accuser. When journalism allows a person to be attacked by anonymous sources, it does not provide this opportunity.

Is it true that certain information cannot be obtained except from anonymous sources? Maybe. But the ethical question still remains: Doesn't the public deserve to have the pertinent information in a story? Certainly in the case of controversial or potentially character-damaging stories, the name of the source would seem vitally important. After all, journalists say they believe in the people's right to know. If they do, then how can they keep something as important as the source secret? The SPJ *Code of Ethics* (1987) reminds us that journalists "must be free of obligation to any interest other than the public's right to know the truth." "Any interest" would surely include the interest of the journalist in keeping a source's identity secret.

Yet, many journalists take great pride in not revealing their sources' names. Some of these journalists have paid fines and even gone to jail for not giving the names of their sources to the court. Some states have "shield laws" that ostensibly protect reporters when they don't reveal their sources. But courts have not always upheld these laws because, in the case of criminal trials at least, the journalist's right to be shielded must sometimes be overridden by the rights of the accused or of the public.

There is no doubt that journalistic sources are important and that journalists must give considerable attention to them: to determining who they will be, how they will be balanced in the story, and whether or not they will be identified. As we proceed now into a discussion of the actual use of material quoted from sources, we should keep the following in mind: If the audience member does not have information (names, occupation, and so forth) about the source of a quotation, the actual quotation loses considerable importance.

This matter of source identification impinges on the most troublesome of the TUFF formula's standards, the final "F" (fairness). To whom shall the reporter be fair? To the source who has been promised anonymity? To the reader who has a theoretical right to know? How does the reporter ensure fairness? This is the *big* question, one that was discussed at some length in Chapter 8.

A Look at Quotations

Once the journalist has decided on a source and has proceeded to conduct an interview with that person, another ethical problem presents itself in the form of two basic questions: What information provided by the source should the journalist select for possible inclusion in the story? and How will the quotations obtained from the source be presented in the story?

Selecting quotations from sources is similar to the problem of deciding what facts, persons, and other details should be included in the story—or which stories should be addressed among all those that are possible. It is a matter of selection, and this process is subjective.

Such subjectivity in obtaining and using quotations automatically gets the journalist into the field of ethics. We have already discussed the problem of truth and objectivity and the journalistic ideal of full-disclosure reporting. The journalist, during and after an interview, is faced with ethical choices: which quotations to use and which to ignore, which ones to play down, and which ones to emphasize. The mere fact of having to select reveals a fundamental (but unavoidable) weakness in the story: incompleteness. In addition, there is the *manner* of presenting what the source says. It is this particular problem—the actual presentation of the quotation—that we turn to now.

Direct or Indirect Quotes?

Once a journalist has someone's statements in note form or on a tape, he or she must decide whether to quote the person directly or indirectly. In other words, should the person's *exact* words be used, enclosed in quotation marks, or should the statement be paraphrased by the reporter, with the quotation marks omitted?

The obvious advantage of direct quotations is that the reader of the story will know precisely the words used by the person quoted. There is no gatekeeper (the reporter) between the person quoted and the reader. Or, at least there is no *translator* interpreting the meaning of what has been said and giving the interpretation to the reader.

Let's assume that a reporter is covering a speech at the White House. At one point President Doe says: "I wish those filthy, stinking pornographers were all confined to hell." Now, that is a direct quotation and it gives exactly President Doe's words. The ethical question is this: Should the reporter give this exact quotation with explicit words that perhaps are not in keeping with the dignity of the office held by Mr. Doe, and which might result in negative consequences for him? Or should the reporter moderate the quotation somewhat while retaining the essential meaning of the actual statement, thereby being fairer to the president? Every journalist is faced daily with this kind of decision. One reporter might have resolved the issue this way: "President Doe said that he wished pornographers were severely punished."

A reporter who would use the direct quote from the president—likely a deontologist—wants to keep the story as close to the truth as possible and is not troubled by possible implications or consequences. The reporter who used the indirect quote wanted to retain the general meaning while shielding the president from unnecessary harmful consequences. This reporter probably had a teleological orientation.

How can such an ethical quandary be resolved? Obviously, different journalists will come to different conclusions. Some will insist on using exactly what the president said. They may reason that a direct quotation informs the readers about an important characteristic of the president that they should be aware of, that it helps objectify the president by showing the kind of words he uses, and that it indicates the *intensity* of the president's feeling about pornography. From the point of view of the objectivist in journalism, it is hard to fault such reasoning. Certainly Immanuel Kant, with his formalistic truth orientation would be proud of such a reporter.

Other reporters would see no reason to use the exact words of the president. For them—the consequence-oriented reporters—the really important thing is to indicate for readers the president's *general concern* about pornography. They feel it is necessary only to project the gist of what he said.

In addition to the deontologist's or teleologist's position in this case, the ethical problem also involves the *distance* from the actuality of the event involved in the two perspectives.

Obviously, the use of the direct quotation, which retains the exact form of the president's sentence, is closer to what *actually* happened and therefore might seem to be superior to a paraphrase. But that conclusion may be the result of mainly *professional* reasoning. Another journalist might well indulge in a different kind of reasoning, one that stressed *ethical* or altruistic considerations and fairness.

For the reporter thinking about fairness and about consequences, there would be no compelling reason to use the president's exact words. For this reporter, there is something more important than being bluntly true, accurate, forthright, and open. This something might go by many names, such as respect, consideration, sensitivity, caring, and concern. For the journalist who would use the indirect quote about the president, an ethical compromise is necessary—one that pulls punches in the name of fairness but retains the basic essence of the quote.

Direct or indirect quotations? Such a question will always be with journalists, who will never all answer the question in the same way. In many cases, journalists shift between direct and indirect quotations without thinking in terms of ethics at all; they are mainly concerned with varying their writing. Using all direct quotations makes for a dull, tedious story, so most reporters alternate direct and indirect quotations. Some of the things sources say are simply said in a dull way. The language-sensitive reporter will try to paraphrase such statements for the sake of readability and will not even be thinking about the relationship to ethics.

Quotation "Patches"

Another problem for the journalist is whether or not (and how) to work partial quotations or "patches" into the context or fabric of the reporter's own language. Here is an example from a hypothetical story:

201

> President Brown, in his talk to the student body of Star-
> light University yesterday, expressed "outrage" at the de-
> gree of cheating and "other unscrupulous student activi-
> ties" that have plagued the university since the fall of
> 1993.
> He recommended that "immediate steps" be taken
> to eliminate from the campus all forms of what he
> termed "disgusting . . . and immoral practices" that have
> "no place in an institution of higher learning."

The practice of using "patch" quotations is designed to
provide the reader with *some* of the source's exact words while
placing these selected bits and pieces in the context of the
reporter's own language. Such a practice opens the door to
ethical problems. The use of partial quotes gives the reporter's
story an impression of reliability, but the impression may be a
false one. Alexander Pope's famous saying that "a little learning
is a dangerous thing" may also suggest that "a little quoting is a
dangerous thing." Partial quotations send a message of credibility and substance, but the message is often built on a wobbly
foundation of misleading connections.

Although it is not evident in our hypothetical story, such
quotation patches can be used to highlight insignificant aspects
of a story or to bring to the reader's attention atypical verbal
mannerisms of the speaker. Such patches may also connect
parts of a speech or an interview which, in reality, were not
related.

Let us look again at the story about President Brown of
Starlight University. First, note the "outrage" in the first sentence. Why is it in quotation marks in the first place? Perhaps
Brown said that he was "outraged," and the reporter parlayed
that into the "outrage" in quotes. Does the "other unscrupulous
student activities" quotation come after his reference to cheating? Actually, the four-word quote may not have been used in
the same context with the cheating to which it is linked; it may
have been used by the president much later in his speech,

when he was talking about students who had been stealing examination papers from faculty offices. Why, we might ask, is "immediate steps" used as a direct quote in the second paragraph? It is not an especially memorable statement, nor is it especially prominent in the story. This may well be a stylistic, not an ethical, consideration. But "immediate steps," like the two patches toward the end of the last sentence, seems to be there only to create an aura of credibility and accuracy. If this is the case, then the partial quotations are unethical in that they attempt to mislead the reader.

Tampering with Quotes

Now we come to a more obvious ethical problem, which has to do with changing direct quotations, actually tampering with the quotes obtained from sources. In a sense, even indirect quotes can be tampered with through patch quotes, with poor paraphrasing, or by quoting out of context. Let us concentrate now on the journalist's practice of actually changing to various degrees what is between the quotation marks.

Some journalists do not think that such tampering is unethical. Jeffrey Olen is one such journalist, now a journalism professor at Pennsylvania State University. Olen (1988, 98) writes that when he was a newspaperman he interviewed many people. He would either tape their conversations or would use a pad and pencil. "Since most people talk faster than I can write," he explained, "the best that I could do was jot down key phrases. Then back at the office I would reconstruct what I heard from my notes—and put the reconstructions in quotation marks."

To Professor Olen, and to other journalists, this is quite permissible. Olen explains his rationale as follows:

> How accurate were these quotes? Accurate enough that I never heard any complaints. Of course, that is not saying

> very much. Few people can remember their exact
> words, and as long as the quotes sounded like what the
> people I'd talked to might have said, they were satisfied.
> In other words, all their satisfaction attested to was my
> ear for dialogue and fidelity to their meaning (98).

Olen's explanation sounds reasonable enough. But there is still an ethical problem—not with the feelings of the persons quoted (he has taken care to say they were satisfied) but with the relationship between the writer and the readers of the story. The readers trust the quotation; they have faith that the people are being quoted correctly, directly, and that the quotes are not just "accurate enough." We take a different perspective: We believe that the integrity of the direct quotation must be retained, that everything between quotation marks and attributed to person-A *must have actually been said by person-A.*

It must be noted, however, that the U.S. Supreme Court has sanctioned the deliberate alteration of direct quotes. In 1991, the Court considered accuracy in quotations in a lawsuit brought by Jeffrey Masson, a psychoanalyst, against *New Yorker* writer Janet Malcolm. She was accused of libeling him by mis-quoting him or by changing what he had actually said and quoting him as if he had said it. Although Malcolm had altered some quotes, the Court concluded that she had not changed the *meaning* of Masson's words, and thus there was no libel. Commenting on the result of this case, Kennedy, Moen, and Ranly (1993, 60) concluded that "most journalists heaved a sigh of relief, although many lamented the Court's seeming endorse-ment of altered—that is, inaccurate—quotes."

Kennedy and his coauthors also refer to an article by Kevin McManus in the *Columbia Journalism Review* in which McManus had interviewed prominent journalists and found that they offered three main ways to handle direct quotes: (1) "clean them up"—correct grammatical errors and omit redun-dant words and such sounds as "uh" and "um"; (2) "make some of it up"—that is, make complete sentences of fragments and fill in partial quotes; and (3) "shape quotes to make them more stylistically acceptable"—tamper with the quotes to make them more readable and memorable (60).

Most journalists would say that falsifying the facts is an absolute taboo. But there is some confusion over just what "the facts" are. William A. Henry III (1993, 54) has written that many reporters "believe it is legitimate to tighten a quote from an interview subject, on the theory that the speaker is appearing in print and would have been more concise if he had written his remarks." But, as Henry points out, other journalists see such tampering with the quotes as "a fabrication."

The matter of changing words or omitting them from a direct quote is certainly a fabrication. As such, the practice is unethical. It is being less than honest with the reader; it is playing fast and loose with the truth; and it violates the trust that should exist between a journalist and the public. Undoubtedly, the issue is not closed, and there will be journalists who continue to see nothing wrong with quote-tampering.

A Look at the Way Quotes Are Attributed

In this last section of the chapter, let us turn our attention to the ethics of attribution. How are the quotes, which have been selected to be used, actually attributed to the source? Can a journalist use unethical attribution techniques to mislead or bias the reader for or against a person who is being quoted? What are some of the main techniques used for attribution bias? We will discuss some of the techniques and implications of attribution, and we encourage students to find examples of attribution bias in current magazines and newspapers.

Earlier we mentioned the ethical questions involved with stereotyping, simplifying, or purposely creating unreal images of people, places, and things. Here we are mainly concerned with the stereotyping of *sources*—persons who are being quoted as saying one thing or another.

In order to illustrate the problems inherent in attribution, we will use a study of three presidents (Truman, Eisenhower, and Kennedy), which was published in 1965 (Merrill, 563–70). Although confined to *Time* magazine and concerned with the broader aspects of biased reporting, the study does indicate how a publication can—through the way it attributes quotations to others—add another dimension to biased reporting. We will concentrate on the *verbs* used to attribute and the *adverbs* used to modify or strengthen the verbs of attribution.

Attribution Verbs

Attribution bias is bias that is caused by the way a publication attributes information to a certain person. In this case of verbs, the bias is contained in the synonyms for the word *said* used in the story. An attribution verb such as *said* is neutral; it is not opinionated and evokes no emotional response from the reader. An attribution verb such as *snapped,* on the other hand, is a word designed to appeal to the reader's emotions, to give a negative cast to the report. An attribution verb such as *smiled* is positively biased or affirmatively affective.

In the Merrill study (568), it was found that Truman (not a favorite of *Time*) in his remarks *barked, cracked, preached, flushed, probed,* and *grinned.* Eisenhower (*Time's* favorite) had his statements attributed to him with such terms as *pointed out, chatted, smiled, observed, noted,* and *remarked.* Kennedy (treated most neutrally by *Time*) simply *said, announced, stated, concluded, suggested, contended, maintained, promised* and *recommended.*

Journalists know that by choosing attribution verbs carefully, they can create a certain image of the speaker; and repeating such verbs over and over gives a stereotypical picture of lasting substance. When a person says something, one reporter can say that he *snarled* it, whereas another reporter might say that he merely *stated* it or even *observed* it. Attribution verbs are obviously very powerful, and although they can—if used skillfully by language-sensitive reporters—add to the *objectivity* or realism of the story, they can easily serve as devices that develop the reporter's biases.

Attribution Adverbs

We must consider adverbs as well as verbs when we discuss the way quotes are attributed to sources. As just noted, verbs are powerful if they are used regularly to depict *the way* someone says something. To make a verbal attribution even stronger, the skilled reporter will *add to* the verb an appropriate and reinforcing *adverb*. In tandem, then, verbs and their adverbs—their strengthening agents—are a powerful linguistic means of creating and perpetuating images of persons.

Adverbial bias, part of the attribution potency of a report, depends on the use of adverbial qualifiers or magnifiers. Adverbial bias sort of reinforces the verb bias already present, as in this example: He [Truman] barked *sarcastically*. By telling *how* a person said something, a journalist can create a favorable or unfavorable impression in the mind of the reader. With such verbs and adverbs, the journalist is actually subjectivizing the story and opening it up to personal interpretation and distortion.

It is interesting that in the presidential study (1965, 565), the attribution verbs were strengthened by adverbs only for Truman and Eisenhower (the villain and hero of *Time*'s reportage), while the verbs used for Kennedy were not modified by adverbs. Let us look briefly at some of the adverbs used for Truman and Eisenhower to strengthen the potency of the attribution verbs.

When Truman did simply say something, *Time* had him saying it *curtly*, or *coldly*, or *slyly*, or *sarcastically*, or *bluntly*. But Eisenhower said *happily*, chatted *amiably*, pointed out

207

cautiously, and said *warmly.* Kennedy, in the reportage of *Time*'s journalists, could only say, suggest, conclude, announce and maintain—with no clue as to whether he was happy, insistent, angry, or whatever.

It should be noted, and this was part of the same study, that attribution techniques other than verbs and adverbs can be used by a publication to create an image. Here is a sample of some subjective expressions used by *Time* in reporting speeches by the three presidents (568):

> TRUMAN: "with his voice heavy with sarcasm"/ "preached the Truman sermon"/ "flushed with anger"/ "made his familiar, chopping motions"/ "publicly put his foot in his mouth"/ "with a blunt finger he probed"/ "was as cocky as ever"/ "petulant, irascible president" /"wore a harried and rumpled air."
>
> EISENHOWER: "said with a happy grin"/"paused to gather thought"/ "with equanimity and inner ease"/ "sensitive to the mood of the nation"/ "had a serene state of mind"/ "frankness was the rule"/ "skillfully refused to commit himself"/ "obviously a man with a message"/ "brushing aside misunderstanding."
>
> KENNEDY: There was no such descriptive reportage relating to his speeches.

A Final Word on Sources

We have seen that the whole area related to sources, their statements, and the way journalists attribute these statements to the sources is complex and ethically troubling. One of the most important ethical concerns is the relationship existing between a journalist and the source. If a journalist is too friendly with a source, there is an automatic inference, whether true or false, of bias.

Journalism professor Gene Goodwin (1983, 114–15) gives

an example of such a friendship in Washington during the Kennedy administration. He mentions that when Roger Mudd was working at CBS he was known to Washington insiders as a friend of the Kennedy family. According to Goodwin, Mudd's friendship with the Kennedys was not much different from the kind of social relationship found among many Washington reporters and high government officials and members of Congress. The friendship did, however, cause Mudd to hesitate about taking on an hour-long documentary for CBS News on Ted Kennedy as a candidate for president. But, relates Goodwin, Mudd did the documentary, and it contributed to the senator's lack of success in getting the 1980 Democratic nomination.

What happened was that Roger Mudd, perhaps to offset the image of being a Kennedy insider, made his questioning so tough that Kennedy's incoherent replies cast the senator in a negative light. Goodwin notes that this program ended Mudd's friendship with Ted's wife and caused a "great freeze to descend on Mudd from Senator Kennedy and his immediate family and staff" (115).

What, we might ask, is the ethical propriety of a journalist having friends who might be sources? The answer: Be careful; do not get close to your sources. You can't avoid them and, in fact, you must cultivate them to the degree that they will trust you and be willing to talk with you. But keep a safe distance. What this distance will be is a journalistic variable; the journalist has to work this out one case at a time. In any event, it is clear that friendship with sources may appear to be a conflict of interest, whether it is or not, and that the journalist must avoid taking chances.

The opposite point in the nexus between journalists and sources is the adversarial relationship. Reporters seem to feel more comfortable with such a relationship, looking on sources as foes who need to be opened up. The contentious type of relationship probably comes from the more general idea that the press and government are in an adversarial relationship. This approach, of course, can be as unethical and counterproductive as the friendship relationship. There is no real reason why a source should be a journalist's enemy, and a reportorial demeanor that suggests that may well cause the source to be uncooperative.

What is perhaps needed in all of this is the use of Aristotle's golden mean—seeking a journalistic position at some distance from the extremes, a moderate and flexible position. Whether we are talking about exposed sources or secret sources, direct quotes or indirect quotes, full-disclosure reporting or selective reporting, we need to realize that these are not either-or questions. Ethical journalists are free to reason through the ethical dilemmas and come to rational and moderate conclusions.

Let us proceed to the final chapter and do a little summing up. We will present a moderate ethical perspective that brings journalistic ethics to a meeting point between communitarianism and libertarianism, a position that is being called ethical mutualism.

ANALYZING ETHICAL ISSUES

1. If a journalist goes to a news source with questions, and this source refuses to answer them or answers them obliquely or obscurely, what should the journalist do? Is it enough to accurately report evasive answers? Why did the journalist choose this particular source in the first place? If a source will not talk to the journalist, should this be part of the story? If your answer is "yes," explain why this should be part of the story. Should all the other relevant sources (who were not interviewed) also be named? Should the method of (and reason for) choosing certain sources be given as part of the story? Explain your answers.

2. The SPJ *Code of Ethics* says that news stories should not be published or broadcast "without substantiation of their claims to news value." How would a journalist substantiate such a *claim* that the story has news value? Would such a claim indicate real news value? Should the journalist determine the news value of a story, or rely on somebody else's claim that it has news value?

3. Would you say that a direct quotation is more truthful and honest than an indirect quote? If so, is it ethical for a reporter to use indirect quotes and be less than honest? Even if a reporter uses direct quotes from a source, does this mean that this part of the story is objective? How might an indirect quote bias or misrepresent what a source actually said? Does *how* (or perhaps *why*) a source says something need to be included in the story? Should attribution verbs (for example, *snapped*, *snarled*, *whispered*) be omitted whenever possible? Why or why not?

4. What are the ethical implications of a reporter using quotation patches (groups of words from a statement or speech used out of context or in loose context)? How can a reporter avoid such a practice? If a reporter gets no complaint from a source about a quote used in a story, does this mean that the quote was ethical? That the quote was accurate? Explain.

5. Washington political reporter-A has lunch with a senator. Reporter-B (who covers agriculture) is a friend of the secretary of agriculture and often goes to his home for dinner or a party. A reporter in the Montana state capital accompanies the governor (on a state airplane) on a trip to Mexico, where the governor is giving a speech. Is there anything ethically wrong with these scenarios? What would you do in each case, and why?

References

Cranberg, Gil. "Journalism Reviews Vary as Much as Newspapers in Using Anonymous Sources." *ASNE Bulletin* (March 1990).

Goodwin, H. Eugene. *Groping for Ethics in Journalism*. Ames: Iowa State University Press, 1983.

Henry, William A., III. "When Reporters Break the Rules." *Time,* 14 March 1993.

Kennedy, George, Daryl R. Moen, and Don Ranly. *Beyond the Inverted Pyramid.* New York: St. Martin's Press, 1993.

Merrill, John C. "How *Time* Stereotyped Three U.S. Presidents." *Journalism Quarterly,* vol. 42, no. 4 (autumn 1965).

Olen, Jeffrey. *Ethics in Journalism.* Englewood Cliffs, NJ: Prentice Hall, 1988.

Society of Professional Journalists. *Code of Ethics.* 1987.

CHAPTER TEN

A SUMMING UP

Our journey, with this final chapter, comes to an end. We have taken a number of interesting highways—ethical theories—through the field of journalism ethics. We have made our way from the pragmatism, egocentrism, and individualism of Machiavellianism, through the intuitivism of the religionists and existentialists, to the virtue ethics of Aristotle and Confucius. In addition, we have studied libertarianism and individualism and the newly formed communitarians, with their aims of social harmony and egalitarianism. It has been, primarily, a journey on the major philosophical highways.

It is hoped that the journey has been a fruitful one. An ethical journey, even a verbal one such as we have just taken, is difficult. Ultimately, the important part of the ethical experience is in the *doing*, in actually putting the concepts into action.

This journey has been wide-ranging. Various perspectives on ethics have been presented, but two have been stressed: the communitarian and the individualistic. However, this two-valued categorization, as the general semanticists point out, is too restricted and simplistic. Thus, we took a deeper look into other syntheses and approaches to ethical behavior: absolutism and relativism, deontology and teleology, rationalism and instinctivism, libertarianism and authoritarianism, objectivity and subjectivity, and a host of other opposites that pull us one way or the other.

Toward an Ethical Mutualism

All of this leads us to a kind of ethical mutualism, which seems to be the best solution for the journalist's ethical quandaries. The various ethical perspectives have been discussed, or at least noted: the strict rule orientation (Kant); the direct intuitive guidance of religious experience (Kierkegaard); the various forms of utilitarianism (J. S. Mill); and Nietzsche's critique of traditional morality. From each ethical theory or emphasis, the journalist can find something of value, and a wise synthesis of the valuable aspects will help each person develop a mutualistic, but personal, ethical philosophy.

As the general semanticists have stressed, the thoughtful journalist will shun the two-valued orientation—the either-or way of thinking. In the *mutualistic* thought process, individualism merges with communitarianism, egoism with altruism, religious sensitivity with scientific concern, rationalism with emotivism, legalism with consequentialism, and absolutism with relativism. In the case of communitarianism and individualism, the historic mega-emphases from which various ethical theories emerge, mutualism is paramount (see Figure 10-1). No person is a secluded atom, and each of us needs the cooperation and company of others. Consequently, we must veer away from the extreme road that leads to anarchy and nihilism and travel the moderate path of respect for society. In like manner, communitarians must not lose sight of the importance of the individual; they must travel the moderate road of responsible use of freedom, so as not to stumble into mass conformity or sink into authoritarianism.

It is hoped that the student has concluded that the Aristotelian golden mean will quite often, if not always, lead the journalist to a more moderate and ethical position. A good example of a philosopher-statesman who can serve as a foundational mentor for such a moderate synthesis is Edmund Burke (see box, p. 216). In the process of stressing a mutualistic and moderate

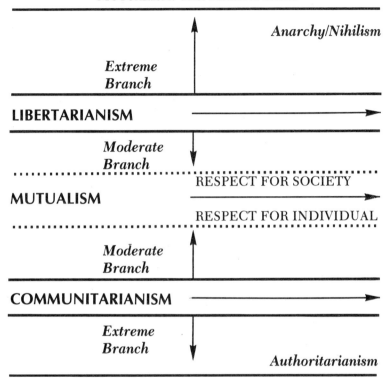

FIGURE 10-1
MUTUALISM: THE MIDDLE ROAD

Anarchy/Nihilism

Extreme
Branch

LIBERTARIANISM

Moderate
Branch

RESPECT FOR SOCIETY

MUTUALISM

RESPECT FOR INDIVIDUAL

Moderate
Branch

COMMUNITARIANISM

Extreme
Branch

Authoritarianism

approach to ethics, we have introduced the main ethical theories and many ideas of various moral philosophers. The whole problem of press freedom and its relationship to ethical journalistic action has been explored, pointing up the fact that freedom can be used ethically as well as unethically.

This book has also stressed what Aristotle understood perfectly: that we become virtuous or ethical—and thereby truly happy—by habitually acting virtuously. We learn to act virtuously in much the same way as the violinist becomes a violinist—by practice, habit, or repetition. Aristotle (1985,

215

Edmund Burke (1729–1797)

The eighteenth-century Irish philosopher and statesman, Edmund Burke, had much to say about responsibility, freedom, and truth—interests of all modern journalists. A person who prized freedom as well as responsibility, Burke did much to synthesize these ideas into a meaningful philosophy. He might be called one of the founders of modern-day mutualism. Since Burke was a liberal thinker who wanted to retain the foundations of civility, manners, and social stability, he represented what is called in this chapter a cautious but enlightened view of change and social progress.

Not wanting a government-controlled media system, Burke would argue that journalism has the basic responsibility to maintain social order and that such maintenance is more important than trying to be fair or objective. Like Confucius and Aristotle, he saw great value in social habits—customs, prejudices, and institutions. One reason Burke opposed the French Revolution was that it sought to uproot basic religious and moral traditions. He looked with suspicion on revolutionary change.

Burke was extremely suspicious of power, and he would urge journalists to expose its misuse, to foster social stability, to stress tradition and civility and to oppose abrupt social change. He would propose that new concepts of journalism, even if made by brilliant thinkers, cannot be as valid as practices that have been viable for many generations.

1103a32–b2) believed that "we become just by doing just actions, temperate by doing temperate actions, brave by doing brave actions." For Aristotle, a good character comes about from the repetition of many small acts, beginning when we are very

continued

For Burke, journalists should be arbiters of good and evil, subtly but consistently determining a nation's value system. Playing up the antics of social eccentrics and sensational episodes designed to titillate and not edify would be anathema to Burke. He would, like the Hutchins Commission of the 1940s, like to see socially relevant, serious, and positive news and views emphasized by the press.

A competitive press system, both among media and within a single medium, would be considered socially beneficial by Burke. He believed that competition encouraged quality and sharpened skills. He would recommend reporting that gave serious attention to historical causes for events and that also pointed out the ramifications of the actions. In short, he was both historical and futuristic in his reportorial philosophy, seeing this as the way to getting closest to the truth.

According to Burke, a concern for ethics would demand that journalists voluntarily decide to curb their natural inclination to freedom. Journalistic self-management would be not only a legitimate practice but a socially responsible one. Burke's basic requirement would be to protect social stability and security and raise the moral and intellectual level of the society. Today, journalists might see such a philosophy as potentially dangerous to press freedom. But Burke was touting a responsible use of freedom, one that had society and its needs as its end.

young. Like Confucius, Aristotle stressed habituation. Training is most important; thinking is a stimulus to acting. Thus, training, thinking, and acting must be fostered for the ethical journalist: "The virtues arise in us neither by nature nor against nature, but we are by nature able to acquire them, and reach our complete perfection through habit" (1103a23–26).

We have seen that Aristotle's view of morality is referred to as the indirect view (Hudson, 1986), in which the emphasis is put on the individual or agent and not on the act itself. This would mean that a journalist with a *moral character* could do an unethical act and still be considered moral. On the other hand, we have seen that many journalists take the direct view of ethics, in which the emphasis is placed on acts themselves and not on the character of the individual. The direct view can be embodied in various ethical theories, such as intuitionism or consequentialism (Hudson, 1986, ch. 2).

A Glimpse at Darker Ethics

A kind of nonmorality or antimorality has been introduced in this book, but it has been dealt with only peripherally, drawing on the ideas of Machiavelli. Perhaps it helps some readers to understand ethics by looking also at pragmatics or non-ethics, the dark side of ethics proposed by the Florentine thinker. We have noted also a kind of supermorality—that of Nietzsche, which stresses alternatively the ethics of success and the ethics of transcendence of conventional values. Undoubtedly, such ideas are appealing to many, but they cannot (or should not) be taken seriously by the conscientious, ethical journalist. Machiavelli, as we have seen, urges conventional morality when it works but advises departing from it, and using more devious methods, if they are needed to bring about desired results. Machiavellianism is not the kind of ethics demanded of journalists who must have the respect and credibility of the public.

For his part, Nietzsche advises us that the "higher man" can overcome traditional morality by eliminating the concept of the good and the just and the normal system of values. There is something arrogant, even authoritarian, in such a view. For

218

Nietzsche, traditional morality damages the creative human drive because morality seeks to prevent diversity and change. Nietzsche thought that the moral tradition results in making past values rule the future, thus preventing an individual's spiritual development (Schutte, 1984, 134). Nietzsche sees future values as being discouraged or considered unwarranted when present or past values are believed to be absolute. Therefore, he reverses society's expectations and assigns values to those concepts that go against social expectations. We can see that Nietzsche would have little in common with the modern communitarians. It is too bad, Nietzsche says, that the conventional ethical wisdom penalizes whoever has the power to create an ethical concept other than that of the ruling ideology (Schutte, 1984, 135). From this radical platform, Nietzsche attacks the notion of moral rigidity. His transvaluation of value is, of course, an extreme form of individualistic ethics and is not consistent with the rational mutualism proposed in this book.

We have purposely given short shrift to the darker sides of ethics exemplified by such figures as Machiavelli and Nietzsche. The lighter ethical perspectives have been emphasized—the Enlightenment and romantic individualism, and social ethics such as communitarianism. We have seen how these two broad ethical perspectives impact upon journalism and how a merger of the two can provide the best moral worldview.

Two Lighter Perspectives

The Enlightenment or individualistic perspective stresses self-development, individual ethical determination, existential risk-taking, pluralism, skeptical reason, and personal freedom. This perspective has the dangerous potential to fall into Machiavellian or Nietzschean excesses, but this need not occur. It is a valuable perspective and should not be shunned by journalists seeking a firm ethical foundation.

The second perspective—that of social ethics—emphasizes communalism, altruism, tradition, social concern, ethical legalism, and conformity. While the individualist stresses a relativistic ethics, the communitarian or social ethicist tries to find common values in order to form a moral community that is cooperative, cohesive, and harmonious.

Rational journalists, those who desire to be ethical, will try to avoid the extremes of both individualism and communitarianism. They will value self *and* community; they will pay attention to self-development and, at the same time, to a cooperative demeanor in society. This is part of ethical mutualism. At the same time, ethical journalists will try to develop a moral character (the indirect view) while they also consider the importance of specific acts in particular situations as they arise (the direct view). This, too, is part of ethical mutualism.

Needed: A Firm Foundation

Although it is easy to despair of the state of journalistic ethics in this country, there is reason to hope that new generations of journalists will have a heightened awareness of their moral responsibilities. A sound ethical foundation in journalism is not easy to acquire. As Arthur Schopenhauer (1788–1860) said: "To preach morality is easy, to give it a foundation is hard." We hope this book provides at least part of the foundation. At this point, we might also remember the words of Albert Schweitzer (1957, 103), one of the twentieth century's foremost ethical leaders:

> Is there . . . any sense in ploughing for the thousand
> and second time a field which has already been ploughed
> a thousand and one times? Has not everything which can
> be said about ethics already been said by Lao-tse, Confu-
> cius, the Buddha, and Zarathustra; by Amos and Isaiah;
> by Socrates, Plato, and Aristotle; by Epicurus and the
> Stoics; by Jesus and Paul; by the thinkers of the Renais-

> sance . . . and of Rationalism; by Locke, Shaftesbury,
> and Hume; by Spinoza and Kant; by Fichte and Hegel;
> by Schopenhauer, Nietzsche, and others? Is there any
> possibility of getting beyond all these contradictory con-
> victions of the past to new beliefs which will have a
> stronger and more lasting influence? . . . We must hope
> so, if we are not to despair of the fate of the human race.

Ethics: Practical and Rational

For the journalist, ethics is a practical problem and a difficult one at that. But the wise journalist will remember that ethical foundations are practical, useful, and have a purpose. Ethics in journalism has to do with "right" (or "better") actions that will accomplish some pragmatic goal, such as leading to a better understanding, bringing more happiness, enlarging the dimensions of truth available to the public, improving social institutions, or pleasing one's god or one's self. If ethics were not practical, we would feel no desire to be ethical. This practicality of ethics, however, must be undergirded by theory, by metaphysical concerns, and by personal commitment.

Although the instinctive, emotive, and religious aspects of ethics have been touched on in this book, there is no doubt that ethics is, by and large, a *rational* enterprise. It generally follows rationally formulated rules or *ad hoc* ethical reasoning; it is not simply a matter of opinion whereby one person's ethics is as good as another's. Ethics is mainly a rational inquiry that tries to reach some unified deductions and conclusions; in this respect, it resembles a science.

As Henry Hazlitt (1972, 6), wrote, "Let us agree . . . provisionally, that ethics is at least one of the 'moral sciences' (in the sense in which John Stuart Mill used the word) and that if it is not a 'science' in the exact and narrower sense it is at least a 'discipline'; it is at least a branch of systematized knowledge or study; it is at least what the Germans call a *Wissenshaft.*"

Part of this "branch of systematized knowledge," the journalistic ideal of truth-telling, has been stressed in this book, along with its fellow concepts of objectivity and accuracy. Considerable attention has been given to fairness and its often contradictory relationship to truth and objectivity. We have also studied propaganda and general semantics, two subjects seldom discussed in journalism ethics books. As an example of more concrete journalistic quandaries, the preceding chapter covered the ethics of dealing with news sources, thus providing the reader with an example of rather detailed moral reasoning.

A Rising Ethical Consciousness

We know from numerous recent surveys that no more than a third of the American people think that journalists have high ethical standards. Things are not good on the ethical front. One reason for this may be that journalists prize their independence and their decision-making capacity. They are, in spite of notable exceptions, generally against being hemmed in by rules. As this book has tried to point out, certain ethical rules are useful. Henry Hazlitt (1972, 183) has said, "Even a rather poor ethical rule is better than no rule at all." Why is this? Hazlitt explains: "This is again because we need to know in our daily actions what to expect of each other, because we are obliged to rely on each other's conduct, and must be reasonably able to count in advance on what the action of others is going to be."

Rules are inherent in ethics. These may be broad rules, or principles, or maxims. But they are guiding moral directives, and they are either internally determined or determined from some kind of peer pressure or historical foundation. Ethics is becoming an increasingly important part of journalism practice and education. Conferences and workshops dealing with media ethics are proliferating, and it is clear that journalistic consciousness has been raised. Whether there is a positive correlation between increased *talk* about ethics and more ethical journalistic *practice* is still unknown, but we can assume that journalists are more aware of their ethical problems.

Even though individual journalists may be developing higher ethical sensibilities, journalism as a whole, unlike the medical and the legal professions, has no minimum entrance requirements, no licensing procedures, no disciplinary panels, and no standardized ethical codes of behavior. Although communitarians are pushing for tougher ethical codes, such ideas have much opposition.

Many journalistic practices that are acceptable to some media—such as the undercover exposure of wrongdoing—are frowned on or forbidden by others. It is still the norm in American journalism for editors to treat each case individually, and this, of course, often means permissiveness or cowardice. In fact, some writers on morality, such as Gertrude Himmelfarb (1995), see the main problem for our age as extreme relativism, in effect having no morality at all. Himmelfarb, a CUNY history professor emeritus in New York City, says that our chief fault is that we are "nonjudgmental."

The Elusive Moral Sense

Journalists, however, are basically judgmental, and they seem to accept some ethical theory, whether they know it by name or not. Regardless of the ethical theory they embrace, journalists tend to have what might be called a moral sense or a conscience. Intellectual fads and fashions, like secular humanism, Marxism, Freudian psychoanalysis, political correctness, postmodernism, deconstructionism, critical theory, and multiculturalism, may confuse or distort one's moral sense, but such fads tend to pass away, and the person retains a basic moral sense.

Most practicing journalists, busy as they are with the mundane problems of their jobs, will probably pay little attention to the great philosophers or to ethicists in today's academic world. Quite likely, they will continue to act out of some kind of internalized moral sense developed in them through the years by their experiences. But the journalism student, not yet saddled with the daily routine of news work, has the time and the opportunity to learn about moral theory and the practice of moral reasoning.

This book, concerned as it is with philosophical ethical foundations, has been directed mainly at students, the future journalists of America. Today's journalists who do, on occasion, read academically based books about the press, may find some intellectual and moral nourishment from the experience. It is hoped that journalism students will be successful in arriving at their own ethical standards and that this book—among others—will aid them in achieving higher ethical levels. It is further hoped that students will recognize their own individual worth, while at the same time appreciating the value of the communities in which they live and work.

ANALYZING ETHICAL ISSUES

1. Do you think it is possible to be an ethical mutualist? How can journalists follow hard-and-fast maxims or rules and also consider the special situation and the consequences of their journalism? If a journalist does try to be an ethical mutualist, which orientation should come first and dominate—the teleological or the deontological? Would the general semanticist approve of mutualistic ethics? Why or why not?

2. What would Aristotle say about a normally moral journalist (a person of "character") writing a story that was generally considered to be unethical, in that it damaged a person's reputation or even put the person in danger? What would John Stuart Mill say? Do you believe that a journalist's character is more important than the

A Summing Up

atypical (negative) acts that he might commit? Would you say that
Aristotle is more of a libertarian or more of a communitarian? Why?

3. Why would Machiavelli's ethics (or at least the ethics that he
recommended) be considered "dark"? Would you consider his pro-
posals to be ethics at all? Why? Do you think many journalists are
Machiavellian in their journalism? Can you give some examples of
such a stance? What is the difference between enterprising reporting (for which awards are given) and Machiavellian reporting?

4. Would Nietzsche be sympathetic to modern communitarians?
Why or why not? Would he take an existentialist position in journalism, for example, championing individualism and freedom? Is
his idea of the "transvaluation of values" (of being one's own deter-
miner of values) a realistic or practical position for modern journalists? Is the Nietzschean stance congenial with Kantian ethics?
Why or why not?

5. Are all ethical decisions made by journalists equal? Why might
some be superior to others? How would a journalist determine
those that were worse, better, best? Is ethical reasoning superior
to intuitive ethics? Are the two necessarily incompatible? How is
it that ethical reasoning often results in contradictory conclusions?
Is ethics a science or a subjective and relative enterprise? Explain.

References

Aristotle. *Nichomachean Ethics.* Translated by Terence Irwin. Indianapolis:
Hackett, 1985.
Hazlitt, Henry. *The Foundations of Morality.* Los Angeles: Nash Publishing,
1972.
Himmelfarb, Gertrude. *From Victorian Virtues to Modern Values.* New York:
Alfred A. Knopf, 1995.
Hudson, Stephen D. *Human Character and Morality.* Boston: Routledge &
Kegan Paul, 1986.
Schutte, Ofelia. *Beyond Nihilism: Nietzsche without Masks.* Chicago: Univer-
sity of Chicago Press, 1984.
Schweitzer, Albert. *The Philosophy of Civilization.* New York: Macmillan,
1957.

APPENDIX

Brief Ethical Issues/Cases for Analysis

Presented below are a number of short ethical cases and issues that can either be discussed in class or assigned as short papers. All of these are based on actual ethical quandaries that are faced by journalists in their everyday work.

1. *A Journalist's Loyalty.* A journalist works for a newspaper and says she has a loyalty to it. The journalist promises a source that she will not use his name. This same journalist believes in the "people's right to know" and therefore has a loyalty to the audience. The journalist also has a loyalty to her government and country and to political and social stability. How would the journalist reconcile such loyalties?

2. *The Unnamed Source.* Should there be unnamed sources in a story? If a major definer of a report is the possibility of verifiability, what does this mean for a story with no named

227

source? Should a reporter promise a source confidentiality? What are some reasons for and against naming sources?

3. *Invading Privacy.* A photographer with a telescopic lens sits atop a hill outside a private beach on the Riviera. He works for a picture magazine in the United States. On the beach is a well-known American movie actress and her boyfriend splashing about in the surf with absolutely nothing on. What should the photographer do? Give reasons for your answer.

4. *Receiving the Gift.* It is Christmas. Bill Smith of the *Sun* has just received a wall clock, a Matisse print, and a bottle of Scotch from Mayor Charles Giver. What should Smith do? Why should he do it?

5. *The One-Sided Story.* It is 3:45 p.m. Reporter Jane Watson is writing a controversial city council story. Her deadline is 4:00 p.m. She has interviewed the mayor, who has blasted Councilman Billings. Watson calls Billings, but he is not in his office. What should reporter Watson do?

6. *The Hidden Identity.* Magazine reporter Berk Shire hears that prisoners are being mistreated in the state prison. The warden either will not talk to the press or seems to be evading the questions. Shire, a very conscientious reporter, decides to commit a crime that will have him sent to the state prison. He hides his journalistic identity from the prison authorities, serves his time, and writes his story exposing the prison excesses. Was Shire's behavior ethical or not?

7. *"Not Available for Comment."* University president Stan Bach is criticized in the student newspaper. One of the faculty members in journalism, Woody Johnson, has said that the president lacks managerial skills and is arrogant in his dealings with the faculty. The student newspaper writes the story, quotes Johnson, and makes a call to the president's office for a response from Bach. The secretary says the president is not in, that he's out of the office. The story is written and appears the next day with this sentence at the end: "President Bach was unavailable for comment." Discuss the ethics of such a journalistic device.

8. *Correcting Errors.* The *Morning Sun* has a front page story

stating that Dennis Ward, police officer, is married. Ward is not married. Should the *Sun* run a correction? Why? If so, when and where in the paper? What kinds of errors should be corrected? How quickly should they be corrected, and how much emphasis should be given to them?

9. *Serving the Public Interest.* Should a journalist serve the public interest? How does she find out what the public interest is? Consider these cases: (1) a governmental official accused of sexual harassment; (2) a cat falling into a deep well; (3) a prostitute arrested in midtown; (4) the discovery of insecticide in the drinking water; (5) a married politician having an affair. How do these stories serve the public interest?

10. *The Staged Photograph.* How truthful should a picture be? A newspaper photographer gets to an award ceremony too late to photograph the actual presentation of the awards. He convinces the participants to reenact the event after the ceremonies have ended. These were not the *real* presentations; they were representations of the event. What are the ethical implications of such a practice?

11. *The Puzzle Quote.* The president is confronted by hostile questions from reporters. He loses his "cool" and snaps: "Get the hell out of here, you goddamned sons of bitches." The *Sun*, in its story the next morning, quotes the president as saying "Get the _____ out of here, you _____ sons of _____." Is this ethical? Is it better or worse than writing "The president, using strong language, told reporters to leave"?

12. *The Doctored Quote.* The reporter is a Democrat. He is covering a speech by a Democratic candidate, who says, in part: "We must keep those right-wing, Fascist bastards among the Republicans from decapitating our welfare system and starving our children." The reporter writes about this in his story as follows: "We must see to it that the right-wing Republicans do not ruin our welfare systems and harm our children's lunch programs." Discuss the ethics of such reporting, even if the reporter had been a Republican.

13. *The Secret Taping.* A reporter interviews a source, taping

the interview without telling the source. Is such a practice ethical? Under any circumstances? How might it be considered unethical? Ethical?

14. *Resurrected Information.* Roger Dodger, the state senator, is running for reelection. The *Sun's* reporter is able to get a short interview with him concerning his beliefs about taxes and abortion, but the senator doesn't say much. The reporter goes to his newspaper's library and pulls out some of Dodger's quotes from two years ago. Some of these old quotes were used in the new story, intermixed with some of Dodger's new quotes. How ethical is such a practice? Discuss the use of resurrected information.

15. *The "Rape Story."* Molly Brown was raped at her high school today. Steve Adams, another student, was arrested and charged with the rape and is in jail. The *Sun* writes the story, giving as many details as it could get, but it did not name the rape victim, Molly Brown. It did, however, name the accused rapist, Steve Adams. What do you think about the ethics of such a story? Look at it from both the teleological and the deontological perspectives.

16. *Paraphrasing.* The governor is making a speech. He has just called a state legislator a "gnat-sized skunk" and a "mealy-mouthed scumbag who is a congenital liar." Reporter Ann Brown is writing the story. In her lead, she writes: "Governor Twinny lashed out at Senator Bill Crowe this morning as he spoke to the legislature, saying that the senator was a contemptible person and a liar." Nowhere did she use the exact epithets of the governor. Is such reporting ethical? What would you have done? Why?

17. *The Omitted Material.* Jack Teller, a reporter for the *News,* takes voluminous notes for a story on a highway accident near Bigtown. He unearthed some information that would lead one to believe that Jack Benson was intoxicated when his car rammed into a school bus. Although there was no hard evidence and no statement from investigating police, several witnesses could be quoted to the effect that Benson "smelled of liquor" and "wobbled" from his wrecked car.

Teller, the reporter, decided to omit from the story the quotes from the witnesses. Discuss this case, giving the reasons why you would or would not leave this material out of the story.

18. *Naming Names.* A *Tribune* reporter covers an attempted bank robbery, which was foiled by Recca Mize, a teller, who pushed an alarm. As the robbers fled, they threatened to kill her. The *Tribune* reporter asked the bank manager for Mize's name, but the manager refused, fearing she might be harmed if her name were known to the robbers. After asking around, however, the reporter got the name and used it in the story. What would have been your decision in this case? Why?

19. *The Free Trip.* The Wellington *Enterprise* is a small, marginally solvent daily newspaper. The editor-in-chief has been asked by the state governor to cover the opening of a newly constructed dam. The governor offered to send a plane to Wellington to fly three *Enterprise* staffers to the dam site. The editor-in-chief accepts the invitation, and the three staffers cover the event. Would you have taken the free trip? Why or why not?

20. *Friend of the Family.* Delia Bell, a Charlotte, North Carolina, television reporter is covering the story of a missing 9-year-old girl. Ms. Bell became a friend of the missing girl's family after the mother had given television interviews to the reporter. Such a friendship made it easy for Ms. Bell to get details of the story unavailable to the local newspaper. It was a cozy arrangement, which helped the television station to get a series of excellent stories and interviews and to win several state journalism awards. Discuss the ethics of such a situation.

GLOSSARY

agenda setting the process, in journalism, of the media determining the events, persons, and ideas the public will be concerned about and will discuss. Traditionally, this has been in the hands of the journalists, but increasingly, audience members themselves are trying to be the agenda setters, as is noted in the rise of public journalism or communitarianism.

Aristotle's virtue ethics an early concept of ethics that emphasized the character or virtue of the person. It stressed a kind of habitual moral activity, that the *person* was ethical (a long-term description), not so much that an *act* was ethical.

attribution bias in reporting, a technique whereby the reporter attributes a quote to a person by using a "loaded" verb, adjective, or adverb. Examples: he snapped, the red-faced speaker, he said curtly.

authenticity in journalism, an existential stance of being one's true self, of living up to one's potential, of lacking hypocrisy and shunning false appearances.

bildung German term (associated with German educator Wilhelm von Humbolt) meaning harmonious individuality nourished by diverse experiences.

Categorical Imperative Immanuel Kant's main ethical principle, which stresses doing what one would like to see universalized. It involves a rational ethics from which various specific ethical decisions stem; it insists that people should always be treated as ends and not as means to some end.

civic journalism a genre of communitarianism, a philosophy that enthrones democratizing journalism by involving the public more in editorial decision making. Also known as *public journalism*.

communitarianism a sociological and philosophical theory or perspective that took a modern shape in the late twentieth century. It is generally attributed to sociologist Amitai Etzioni and emphasizes reestablishing harmonious communities in which basic democracy can better function. In journalism, the emphasis is on the media ascertaining what the people want and giving it to them.

conscience a subjective mental guide, developed through experience and personal insights, that serves as a moral indicator of right and wrong. Also known as a *moral sense*.

deontological ethics legalistic or formalistic ethics. It is exemplified by Immanuel Kant's *a priori* duty ethics whereby a moral agent is bound to follow definite moral principles and not be concerned about possible consequences. Contrast with *teleological* ethics.

dialectic in journalism, a clash of ideas or extremes (thesis and antithesis) resulting in a merger or synthesis, thereby forming a more moderate or more advanced position. It is loosely related to Aristotle's golden mean.

egoistic ethics a philosophy that uses the self as the moral reference point. It ignores outside considerations in making ethical decisions; is concerned with self-development and self-determination; uses reason for personal growth and character development; and rests on the belief that morality can be explained in terms of rational self-interest, which is ultimately in the interest of society.

emotive ethics the belief that ethical terms do not describe anything but are simply expressions of the person using them. For example, saying "X is good" is only saying that "I like X." Such an ethical statement is nothing more than a report of a person's emotional state.

Enlightenment liberalism an emphasis on individualism, competition, and freedom of expression manifest in Europe (especially Britain and France) during the seventeenth and eighteenth centuries. Key figures in the Enlightenment were Milton and Locke in England, and Constant and Montaigne in France. This liberal spirit carried over into America with Jefferson, Madison, and other Founding Fathers, and into the nineteenth century with such thinkers as John Stuart Mill. Also called the Age of Reason.

epistemology the science and study of knowledge. In journalism, it involves a special concern with truth, fact-gathering, and objectivity.

etc. principle in general semantics, the abbreviated way of thinking about the concept of non-allness. For example, the journalist always leaves information out of the story; there is more that could be said; one can never say everything about anything.

ethical mutualism a synthesis ethics that combines a respect for legalistic or deontological ethics *and* teleological or consequentialist ethics. The journalist has a set of basic guiding principles to follow but deviates from them when the highest moral good demands it. A journalist may respect self and journalistic autonomy and at the same time recognize the value of others in a community.

existential journalism an individualistic orientation that stresses freedom, commitment, action, and personal responsibility. It is related to the individualism and subjectivity of romanticism and Enlightenment liberalism. The journalist creates the self by choosing and acting.

flux in general semantics, a basic concept that all is change, all is movement; that reality is constantly changing, but language is more or less static; that everything is becoming and nothing is. An early proponent was the Greek philosopher Heraclitus, who pointed out that no person could step in the same river twice.

freedom in journalism, roughly synonymous with autonomy. It includes the freedom of news media from outside control (*press* freedom) and the freedom of individual journalists from institutional, media direction (*journalistic* freedom). Freedom in both senses is always limited, even in the most libertarian countries.

general semantics a multivalued or non-Aristotelian linguistic orientation, founded by Alfred Korzybski in the early twentieth century. It emphasizes the dynamism of reality versus the static nature of language. It also stresses the individualism of entities and the fact that we cannot say everything about anything. It is mainly concerned with language and its impact on thought, and on thought's impact on action.

golden mean Aristotle's philosophy of moderation in a person's life. It is seen as the rational and virtuous course between extremes, such as too much freedom (anarchy) and too little freedom (slavery). It was strongly proposed as a basic philosophy by Confucius.

hedonism a belief that the highest goal and the greatest good is pleasure.

humanism a philosophy that historically has a spirit of optimism about human potential, enthusiasm about human achievements, and a belief in God. In the twentieth century, the meaning has changed somewhat to include those who reject all religious beliefs. The emphasis now is a concern for human welfare. Often called *secular humanism* in contrast to the earlier religious humanism.

Hutchins Commission a group (officially called the Commission on Freedom of the Press) comprised of Robert Hutchins and twelve commissioners who studied the American press during World War II. They concluded that the U.S. press was basically irresponsible and needed drastic reform along the lines they suggested. Their report met with much press opposition, but it has made a huge impact on journalistic thinking and is related to the rise of communitarianism and an emphasis on social ethics.

idealism Plato's philosophical view that an ideal (perfect idea) exists somewhere for every concrete entity—that what we actually see are no more than imperfect manifestations of the perfect or ideal thing. It is also a philosophy of hope, of human struggle toward perfection, and involves a belief in personal and social progress toward an ideal world. It is often contrasted with realism (a more pragmatic and materialistic perspective).

ideology a general term for any system of ideas and norms directing political and social action, such as Marxist ideology or capitalist ideology.

Glossary

individualistic ethics an ethics in journalism that emphasizes personal or inner-directed decision making and behavior. It is related to Enlightenment liberalism and existentialism. It is not necessarily egoistic, since personal interests and values largely dictate good relationships with others.

inner-directed ethics a self-determined, individually conceived ethics, in which the journalist is directed in ethical matters by his or her own values and wishes.

intuitionism in ethics, the view that moral judgments are known to be true or proper by intuition, that a kind of mystical, nonrational sense or feeling informs us as to what is right and wrong.

justice an ethical concept having to do with providing the proper results to people. It includes the idea of being fair, of providing equal treatment or outcomes, and of giving people what they deserve. Naturally, concepts of justice vary widely among people.

libertarian journalism a personal, individualistic, largely autonomous journalism stemming from eighteenth-century Enlightenment thinking. Freedom of expression is paramount, on both personal and institutional levels. It includes a suspicion of, and reluctance to embrace, any form of outside control or coercion in journalistic activities. There is also a belief in the value of competing messages and the widest pluralism possible in public discourse.

Machiavellianism in journalism, a pragmatic demeanor whereby the journalist's main guiding force is success. Use normal ethical techniques if they work, but don't be afraid to use any means to achieve your end if you believe such an end is a good one. It is derived from the fifteenth-century Florentine adviser and thinker, Niccolò Machiavelli, whose ideas are largely elucidated in *The Prince*.

moral agent the person involved in an ethical decision and action; the one who determines the right or better ethical action on the basis of some moral theory or considerations.

multivalued orientation a primary concern of general semantics, also known as the non-Aristotelian orientation. It emphasizes subtle distinctions in language, a kind of "spectrum thinking" that goes beyond

237

Glossary

two-valued thinking in antonymic categories, for example, tall/short,
liberal/conservative. Considered a more sophisticated and scientifically specific orientation.

negative freedom a concept of freedom that stresses the lack of control, direction, restraint, or guidance from outside the person or the
medium. It is the freedom from external direction, in contrast to *positive* freedom, which is freedom used to do some positive social good.

normative ethics directive or guidance ethics in which specific laws,
rules, norms, or principles are used to guide or direct ethical action.

objectivism the belief that meaningful and reasonably accurate statements can be made about reality. It is the opposite of subjectivism or
idealism, and it includes the belief that reality is sufficiently describ-
able to rational people. It also includes the assumption that certain
moral truths remain true regardless of what anyone might think about
them.

objectivity in journalism, a relationship between symbol (language)
and reality with virtual correspondence of meaning, or harmonizing,
being the result. It is usually designated as a journalistic stance of
neutrality, dispassion, and lack of bias.

PASID formula an acronymic formula or definition for propaganda.
The letters stand for persuasive, action oriented, selfish, intentional,
and devious/deceptive.

people's right to know a basic belief in American journalism, often
justifying the press's excesses in getting and printing what it wishes.
There is no constitutional right to know, but in the context of our
governmental theory, there is a philosophical right for the people to
know at least certain things about the government so that they can be
better citizens.

potential truth the level of truth that the journalist may reach or
access; the aspects of truth that filter from the *transcendental* level
and are available for the reporter to ascertain. Potential truth is the
highest of the journalistic levels of truth, followed by *selected* and
reported truth.

Glossary

pragmatic ethics not generally considered ethics at all but rather a kind of pragmatic justification for certain actions. It is also known as Machiavellian ethics, in which what is considered to be a good end may be pursued by any means.

propaganda an attempt by a person or institution to persuade, to solidify opinion, and to cause a certain action, usually by distortion or providing less than the truth. Propaganda is persuasive, action oriented, selfish, intentional, and deceptive or devious.

propaganda devices seven standard methods listed in the 1930s by the U.S. Institute for Propaganda Analysis. The devices are name-calling, testimonial, transfer, card-stacking, glittering generalities, plain folks, and bandwagon. Others include the big lie, repetition, and false analogy.

rationalism in a narrow and specific sense, the doctrines of a group of European philosophers (including Descartes, Locke, and Leibniz) of the seventeenth and eighteenth centuries. In a broader sense, rationalism involves using reason alone to learn about the nature of existence; the belief that everything is explainable; and the belief that only those things having a rational explanation can be believed.

semantics the science and study of meaning. In journalism, it involves a special concern with diction, with choosing the proper words to communicate the correct or most accurate messages.

situation ethics a relativistic ethics in which one considers the specific situation when determining the action that is ethical. It stands in contrast to absolute or universal ethics.

subjectivism in ethics, a belief that all moral beliefs are merely personal opinions or matters of taste. In journalism, it is the injection of personal opinion or bias into a story and departing from hard facts and the neutral depiction of reality (*objectivity*).

teleological ethics consequentialist ethics; the theory that the rightness or wrongness of an action is dependent on the results or consequences of the act. Contrast with *deontological* ethics.

Glossary

two-valued orientation in general semantics, the normal (and unrealistic) stance toward thinking. It involves the either-or kind of thinking, thinking in antonyms, such as hot or cold, beautiful or ugly, tall or short. The general semanticists recommend a *multivalued* orientation, which they consider a kind of spectrum thinking that is far more discriminating.

utilitarian ethics an altruistic version of *teleological* ethics. It focuses on what will bring the greatest happiness (good) to the greatest number. It is associated with the utilitarian philosophers of nineteenth-century England, particularly James Mill and his son, John Stuart Mill.

INDEX

241

Index

communitarianism, 4–5, 12,
15–16, 21–23, 52–53, 57
community emphasis in, 38–
40
Confucianism as early form
of, 83
libertarianism and, not mutually exclusive, 32–33,
215, 220
overview, 34–38
confidential sources, protecting,
185
Confucius, 34, 54, 83–85, 90,
217
conscience, 56
consequences-oriented reporters, 179–81, 184. *See
also* teleological ethics
constituent groups in society,
presenting representa-
tive picture of, 17–18
cooperationists, 34. *See also*
communitarianism
correction of errors, 183, 186

darker ethics, 218–19
democracy and the press, 2, 7,
10, 80–82, 94. *See also*
press freedom and ethics
Democracy in America, 94
deontological ethics, 55–56, 62–
66, 74, 176, 200
de Tocqueville, Alexis, 93–95
direct view of ethics, 53–54
disinformation, 133
duality of emphasis in journalism ethics, 32–35. *See*

also communitarianism;
libertarianism
duty ethics. *See* deontological
ethics

eclecticism, 99–100, 158–60
educational function of reporting, 184–85
egocentric pragmatics, 57, 72
Enlightenment liberalism, 3–6,
34, 44, 219
communitarian view of, 38–
39
perspectives on press freedom, 89–92, 101–2. *See
also* press freedom and
ethics
See also libertarianism
epistemology, 117–18
equitability, 187–88
errors
correction of, 183, 186
willingness to admit, 183
"etc. concept" (non-allness),
157, 163, 168
ethical development, stages of,
28–30
ethical mutualism, 214–18
ethical theories
altruistic ethics, 63, 66
communitarianism. *See*
communitarianism
darker ethics, 218–19
deontological ethics, 55–56,
62–66, 74, 176, 200
direct and indirect views, 53–
54

242

Index

Index

Index

247